The Mother of Eve —
as a First Language Teacher

MONOGRAPHS ON INFANCY

Lewis P. Lipsitt, Editor

The Mother of Eve — as a First Language Teacher

Ernst L. Moerk

Department of Psychology
California State University, Fresno

with a commentary by
Donald M. Baer

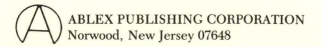

ABLEX PUBLISHING CORPORATION
Norwood, New Jersey 07648

Printed in the United States of America.

Library of Congress Cataloging in Publication Data

Moerk, Ernst L.
    The mother of Eve—as a first language teacher.

    (Monographs on infancy)
    Bibliography: p.
    Includes index.
    1. Children—Language—Case studies. 2. Mother and child—Case studies. 3. Interpersonal relations—Case studies. I. Title. II. Series.
LB1139.L3M655   1983   372.6   82-16358
ISBN 0-89391-163-3

ABLEX PUBLISHING Corporation
355 Chestnut Street
Norwood, New Jersey 07648

Contents

Acknowledgments

This study could not even have been begun without the magnanimity of Prof. Roger Brown, who so willingly and generously lent his valuable transcripts to the investigator although he knew that the main goal of the study was to reevaluate his findings and, if needed, to improve upon them. My profound appreciation is expressed both in the ready acceptance of many of his path breaking insights and conceptualizations, as well as in the criticism of some of the conclusions he reached. Only strong foundations are worth building upon. The quite extensive work undertaken to analyze the wealth of information in the transcripts was made possible by the generous financial support of the Spencer Foundation. Without the means it provided for more intensive concentration upon this research by the main investigator, and for the employment of research assistants, the analyses would have to have been much more restricted. The help of the following research assistants is gratefully acknowledged: Kitty Lou Varney, David R. Cross, Eric G. Don-Pedro, and Janice A. Mathiasen (in the order they joined the project). A final word of appreciation goes to Bev Karau, for her selected stylistic improvements and for the excellent and efficient typing of the long manuscript with its large number of tables.

Preface

The verbal exchanges taking place between mothers and their infants are of celebrated fascination to child development researchers and psycholinguists. Seldom are the processes as meticulously studied, quantified, and thoughtfully explicated as in this remarkable piece of work by Ernst L. Moerk. The report of these data, so obviously important for an understanding of the interactional patterns involved in the reciprocal instigation of vocal utterances, helps us to see more clearly, during linguistic development, the power of corrections, pattern drills, simple repetitions, and other instructional techniques.

A departure from our previous style in this *Monographs on Infancy* series involves the inclusion of a reply by Dr. Moerk to the Commentator on the volume, Donald M. Baer. As it turned out—not for the first time in publishing history—the Commentator, while generally friendly to the research undertaken here, nonetheless urged the author (and others carrying out descriptive research relating to language development) to move quickly into what he believes to be the next stage of research in this important area. Dr. Baer's Commentary was the start of an exchange between the author and himself. We have chosen to publish Dr. Moerk's reply to Dr. Baer's interesting cautionary note. Scholarly service sometimes entails the airing of reservations, argument, and counter-argument. I hope that the repartee included here will provide such a service, and that the helpful dialogue might continue.

The Monographs constitute one component of a tripartite publishing program on infancy begun in 1978 by Ablex Publishing Corporation under my editorial direction. Another part is the journal, *Infant Behavior and Development*, in its sixth volume as this monograph appears, and under the Editorship of Carolyn Rovee-Collier. The third part is *Advances in Infancy Research*, the first volume of which appeared in 1981, and the second in 1983.

The relatively brief research articles appearing in the journal are nicely complemented, we hope, by the two other styles of publication. The *Advances* are intended for intermediate size manuscripts which are critical syntheses of specialized research areas, usually capitalizing upon, but not limited to, the results of the authors' own programmatic research. The *Advances* are intended as collations of data and inferences, not principally as repositories of primary data which are best submitted to journals. The *Monographs*, on the other hand, are for longer manuscripts and usually will report original data. They are also for reports of extended research programs and collaborations. All three publication styles involve editorial scrutiny, including judgments of research experts other than the Editor. In the *Monographs* series, comments by other experts in the area circumscribed by the Monographs are solicited to provide the basis of a Foreword or of a concluding Commentary or both.

We welcome and will review seriously good innovative ideas that report or promote progress in the scientific study of infant behavior and development. We will not be bound by any traditions that do not yet exist. Our policy is to attract and publish high quality manuscripts which will be reviewed and commented upon by established experts on infancy.

Lewis P. Lipsitt, Editor
Department of Psychology, and
Child Study Center
Brown University
Providence, R. I. 02912

The Mother of Eve—
as a First Language Teacher

INTRODUCTION

Contrary to its first impression, the title is intended to be fully informative both as far as its denotative and connotative meaning is concerned. It introduces the sample and its size, namely one dyad. It specifies that the emphasis will lie upon the mother in contrast to the child "Eve," who was studied and reported upon so extensively by Roger Brown during the sixties and the early seventies. The term "a first language" is intended to suggest that many of the bases and the questions for analysis are drawn from Brown's (1973) book of the same title. The title also specifies the topic of discussion as one type of maternal behavior, i.e., the teaching of the verbal code. In linguistic terms, the teaching of the surface structures and of the morphophonemic component are the centers of attention. That the child has acquired meaning-structures underlying her messages is presupposed. That these meaning-structures are acquired in a manner different from the code is considered highly plausible, but their acquisition will not be analyzed. Finally, the title signifies a strong theoretical stance indicated by the term "teacher." It will be attempted to show that the input provided mainly by the mother is rich enough to account for language acquisition, i.e., code acquisition, presupposing an independently acquired cognitive and meaning structure. The emphasis upon teaching is, however, not equivalent with a narrow allegiance to a specific school. Since cognitive, communicative, pragmatic/motivational, and learning aspects are involved, it is presumed that one single and narrow theoretical system cannot exhaustively explain all pertinent phenomena. Concepts will therefore be freely borrowed from the various cognitive, social learning, ethological, and even behavioristic schools.

The title is intended to be informative also in regard to its deemphases and omissions. The child and her learning strategies will generally be deemphasized in the present study. Eve's utterances will be mainly of interest as an occasion for the mother's linguistic intervention and to a minor degree as evidence for the effectiveness of these maternal interventions. Input from other persons is deemphasized too. Why it can be discounted for the present study will be discussed in the Method section.

After the title, and with it the goals of the study, have been preliminarily explicated, they need to be briefly put into perspective. The merest sketch of a survey over research from the last quarter century shall provide this perspective: Skinner (1957) attempted to apply consistently a simplified learning approach to the task of language acquisition. His attempt fell quite obviously short, compared to the complexity of language for which his tools were simply not adequate. Chomsky in 1959 and in all his later publications emphasized this complexity and the fact that Skinner's approach was unsatisfactory. He therefore threw in the towel and, instead of trying to explain language acquisition, took recourse to a miraculous innate device which he posited as functioning on a high level of complexity while the young child was otherwise still struggling with relatively simple cognitive tasks. A somewhat indirect response to Chomsky was elaborated during the seventies in demonstrating that the maternal language input is not extremely complex and that it contains many features which might make verbal communication easier for the child. Most of these studies did, however, not go far enough to demonstrate how this input is related to the children's own verbal output and their language acquisition. Most recently—and perhaps as a reaction to this unsatisfactory approach—Maratsos and Chalkley (1979) and McWhinney (1978) have tried to explain language acquisition by focusing almost exclusively upon the possible cognitive processes of the child. Thereby they have completely neglected the input aspect and have consequently burdened the infant and young child with highly complex strategies and sequences of strategies. Since an assumption of highly complex strategies quite clearly is in contrast to established knowledge about the slow progress in the cognitive development of infants and children, the danger that this approach will lead to explanatory failures and a relapse into nativism is great indeed. By completely neglecting the input aspect, those recent studies are also in the somewhat absurd situation of trying to explain an effect, i.e., the processes and products of language learning, without considering its cause, i.e., the input. Such a procedure would be comparable to the study of second language learning in various classrooms or schools whereby only the behavior of the pupils is considered, and the textbooks and the oral instructional techniques are completely neglected. The investigators would then find that some groups of children rattle off lists of declensions, others converse haltingly and incorrectly, and other classes again perform etymological and grammatical analyses. Great astonishment over these differences might then arise.

In contrast to these recent attempts, the present emphasis lies almost completely upon the input. The interest centers not only upon the simplifications of the input that support the interaction process and that have been summarized so often. It lies more upon the instructional qualities of this input and its instructional consequences. It will be shown how the mother takes messages apart, rearranges their parts, replaces some, and provides redundancy in others in order to make the language code less transparent and the nature of the code more obvious. Since the preceding sentence could be misconstrued as invoking intentional language-teaching on the side of the mother, the topic of intentionality and with it the concept of "teaching" need to be considered briefly. It is not asserted that mothers never teach linguistic skills intentionally, but instructional intentionality is seen as irrelevant in most instances of teaching and learning. To support this assertion, the three most typical situations in mother-child communication that contribute to language acquisition shall be briefly considered:

(a) The mother has to convey a message to the child who does not yet know its content. In this case the meaning structure is unknown and parts of the message structure are often unknown or not readily accessible to the young child. An equation with several unknowns exists that can obviously not be solved. This is the most difficult case the mother and child encounter. It will be shown in the main body of the study how the mother solves this problem. She provides basically a system of several equations in order to make a solution possible. That is, she reformulates her message in several ways, replacing elements, simplifying structures, or employing a variety of structures while maintaining some identical elements in order to increase the chances that the child might be able to analyze the message. It will be seen how successful she is in this endeavor, but also how astonishingly often the endeavor fails despite the employment of versatile instructional techniques. What the mother intends is to convey a message and she explicates the syntactic/semantic structure to achieve this.

(b) Normally the situation is a good deal simpler: The child shows through her nonverbal behavior that she has perceived and conceived a situation, and the mother provides the linguistic equivalent to this cognitive–meaning structure. This is a rather simple task in the case of one-word naming. In the case of the subsequent two-word utterances, one of the two words is often well known to the child, so that only one unknown remains. Once the child has progressed further, the mother can, of course, invite the child to provide the linguistic encoding of the observed situation and can improve, expand, or simply praise the child's product. The main intention is again centered upon verbal communication, though the goal to convey verbal skills may be less indirect than in the first case.

(c) If the mother responds to the child's utterance, the easiest task is encountered: The child has conceptualized a message and has uttered it, even if in a somewhat incomplete or incorrect manner. The mother needs now to make only minor improvements, which, being fitted into the child's cognitive and message structure, can easily be incorporated by the latter. Similarly, as Collis and Schaffer (1975) have shown it for the nonverbal realm, it will be reported in the present study for the verbal realm that the mother accepts and follows with few exceptions the conversational topic begun by the child, so that case (c) is most common in verbal interactions between mothers and their children. It could also be demonstrated that at least the mother of Eve is normally attuned enough to the capacities of her child to provide only few improvements per instance of feedback. In this way, she probably stays within the information processing limits of her child. If she sometimes misses the mark, she receives immediate feedback in the form of a breakdown in the flow of the interactions. In this last case, language instruction is relatively pure, though the mother might only be aware of the discrepancy between the child's utterance and her own standard.

It might appear now that the claims raised are too strong, i.e., that language teaching and learning is not differentiated from noninstructional/ nonlearning verbal exchange. This lack of distinction is fully intentional. Two arguments are pertinent to support it: First, it is quite impossible to predict when children might learn from input. Nor could it easily be proven that they had not learned from it, as research on latent and incidental learning suggests. As every second-language-learner knows from personal experience, much learning results from mere exposure to input without immediate overt language production. The second consideration is that input has effects even after initial mastery. The gradual transition of language mastery from the early receptive competence, to productive accessibility of items, to their ready availability, and finally to their habitual use (Brown, 1973; Fraser, Bellugi, & Brown, 1963) suggests that input remains effective even after initial acquisition. Even after complete mastery, the partial or complete forgetting of one's mother tongue, if it is never used, shows that input and use have a necessary reinstatement function, counteracting natural forgetting.

In conclusion: The learning opportunities provided for the child will be analyzed. This implies that almost all the input is relevant. Rare exceptions to this rule would be short asides, addressed to the observer and inaudible for the child, or utterances that were so complex that the child could not analyze anything of their structure. In the interactions of Eve and her mother, both these types were extremely rare, since the mother was quite well-attuned to her child's level and since most remarks to the observer were clearly audible and also comprehensible for the child, as demonstrated by the fact that Eve repeatedly responded to a remark addressed by the mother to an observer.

METHOD

The entire range of data collected for Eve and her mother was included. Eve was between 18 and 27 months old when the recordings were made; her

MLU ranged from between 1.39 to 4.22 morphemes. Of the 19 samples collected by Brown, all odd-numbered ones were analyzed. Two hours for each of these samples were included. For some analyses, all early samples and all the hours per sample were used. Those hours were chosen for intensive analysis that were longer and in which the observers were relatively quiet. If observers took over the conversation for brief stretches, the section was omitted from the analysis. Rare and brief responses by the observers or the father were, however, included since they often served the same function and followed the same principles of feedback provision as maternal interactions and since their omission would have interrupted the flow of conversation.

Qualitative Aspects of the Analysis

The nature of the data, together with the goals of the study, guided the choice of methods. The main units of analysis are individual utterances. For each utterance in an interaction, three levels are normally differentiated: the level of the meaning or content of the utterance; the illocutionary level, or the goal that the utterance is to fulfill; and the level of the code, encompassing phonetics, phonology, morphology, and syntax. Utterances and language in general can be, however, and often are considered from a fourth perspective. The most general term for it is style. A more narrowly delimited aspect of it has recently been discussed under the terminology "code switching." For the present study, the instructional style that is employed by the more advanced speaker of a language and that makes it easier for the less advanced one to comprehend the structure and content of the message is most important. It will be referred to as "maternal teaching techniques," "teaching techniques," or simply "techniques." This aspect is systematically differentiated from the style that is employed by the less accomplished speech partner in trying to utilize his language skills at least well enough to convey an intended message. These aspects of the child's speech are referred to as "strategies" or "learning strategies." This differentiation is mostly not made in the literature, but it was found to be useful in the present report to refer unambiguously and parsimoniously to the speech of either partner. It certainly conforms quite well to the general educational and psychological use of the terms.

These four major aspects of each utterance are described in the subsequent pages, as they are more or less finely differentiated. Having differentiated these sets and their members, various quantitative analyses could be performed on them as they will be summarized in the last part of the Methods section. before these details are focused upon, the overall design of the study as it is reflected in the computer codings is presented in Table 1.

Due to the intensive and extensive analyses that are planned, a full computer card is reserved for each single utterance. The first four items and the last two on the computer card are self-explanatory and no comment is needed

TABLE 1

The Outlay of the Computer Card, Enabling a Quite Exhaustive Coding of Each Single Utterance

Columns:	1 + 2,	3 + 4,	5 + 6,	7 + 8,	9 + 10,	11 + 12,	13 + 14,	15 – 20,	21 – 66,	67 – 74,	75 – 80
Content of columns	Dyad code	Sample	Hour	Page	Person speaking	Episode boundary	Illocutionary force	Strategies/ techniques	Instructional content	Date and time	Utterance number

in regard to them. Persons speaking are in the present transcripts the mother, code 01, the father, code 02, the child, code 03, and the observers, code 06. In the Result section, all codes will be referred to in their more common form, that is, without the preceding zero. Since both the father's speech and the few utterances of the observers that were included were very infrequent as compared to the utterances of the mother and the child, the results will be discussed in terms of mother-child or child-mother interactions. The child employs "strategies" and "the mother," including father and observers, employs "techniques." The major sets beginning with code 11/12 in Table 1 will be discussed in separate subsections.

(a) *Episode boundaries.* The coding for episode boundaries has several functions in the present study. First, they are the only means employed to deal—even if superficially—with the content of the interactions. They can therefore indicate which of the partners leads the conversation as far as content is concerned, and also how marked the differentiation between leader and follower is. The more important function of the episode boundaries is, however, methodological and theoretical. To explain this, the nature of the episodes and their boundaries have to be considered.

The concept of a verbal behavior episode was employed in previous studies (Moerk, 1972, 1976a). It has been derived from the research of Barker and Wright (1955) on the structures observed in nonverbal behavior. Behavior episodes and sub-episodes are defined to cut up the stream of behavior into sections that have greater internal consistency, and to differentiate those

TABLE 2
The Categories Employed to Code Episode Boundaries

Computer code	Category heading
00	Uncodable
01	No topic
02	Same topic
03	New topic
04	Minor change in the topic.[a]
05	Return to a preceding topic after an intervening digression

[a]Replacement of one content item (constituent) in the message sequence is *not* enough to code 04 (instead of 02). At least two content items have to be replaced to code 04 or 03.
  e.g., Drink water
       Drink juice = 02
But: Drink water
      Eat apple during meal topic = 04
and:
      Talk about meal
      Talk about event in the past = 03
      Talk about eating an apple = 05

from often quite abrupt transitions. To do this, at least two codes are required, one representing a continuing and relatively unchanged topic and the other representing the beginning of a new topic. In Table 2 and for the present study, these are the codes 2 and 3, respectively. Code 3 represents thematic leadership, code 2 thematic following. Complex as verbal behavior even between a mother and her young child is, however, these two codes can not suffice to deal satisfactorily with the variety of topics and subtopics encountered. Minor changes in the topic of discussion are often apparent, as when during a discussion about a meal the theme shifts from the eating of solid foods to the drinking of fluids. Code 4 was therefore introduced to make it possible to record minor changes in topic. The footnote in Table 2 specifies how this code was differentiated both from code 2 and code 3. Both in nonverbal and verbal behavior, returns to a preceding topic are often found after a digression. Code 5 is employed to record this phenomenon. Finally, two wastebasket categories serve to deal with the rest of the utterances encountered that could not be classified under one of the main categories: Brief exclamations, greetings, and other almost contentless utterances were coded as 01, No Topic. The frequent instances when utterances could not be understood by the transcriber and were only indicated by dashes were coded as 00, Uncodable.

Though nowhere approaching the semantic diversity of actual verbal interactions, the subdivisions resulting from this set of codes make it possible to render the semantic rhythm of the interactions. Indicating the breaks in the smooth flow of the themes, these codes can be employed as guidelines for the differentiated computation of transitional probabilities between utterances and the joint probabilities of utterance-pairs. These can be computed both over the entire hour without considering thematic changes, and also separately within the episodes and subepisodes. These separate computations in turn can help to test a preliminary hypothesis derived from a previous study (Moerk, 1976a). Less systematic analyses then gave rise to the impression that minor changes in topic might signal linguistic/thematic "repair sequences," that is, that something in the interaction was less than acceptable—mostly for the mother—and that she therefore produced some variations around the theme to explicate and improve the verbal communication. If transitional and joint probabilities are computed separately for the various episode stretches, a comparison of the results also makes it possible to estimate in how far the lack of stationarity encountered in verbal interactions might distort the results obtained in employing Markov models, which presuppose stationary probabilities.

(b) The illocutionary force. Both lay terminology and philosophical analyses (Searle, 1965, 1969) have established well-proven systems to categorize the illocutionary aspects of utterances. These systems only needed to be partly refined and adapted to the special goals of the present investigation. Table 3 presents the categories of illocutionary force that proved fine enough to differentially categorize most utterances. To code exhaustively all utterances, two waste-basket categories were included with the codes 99 and 00. The differentiation between the categories was well-enough established to make it possible to attain at least 80% intercoder reliabilities. Most of the reliabilities computed separately for randomly selected hours fell into the middle nineties.

Since the detailed explanations of the various codes are given in Table 3

TABLE 3
The Categories Employed to Code the Illocutionary
Force or Conversational Function

Computer code	Categories plus definitions
01	*Declarative*[a] sentence/utterance: Descriptive/intentional, e.g., I'll be right back. Can also be a declarative imitation.
02	Expresses *agreement* through a sentence/phrase that is not standard, e.g., not that's right. If the phrase follows a YES, then it is in all probability an agreement and not 01. Imitations are often employed conversationally to signify agreement.
03	Expresses *disagreement* through a sentence/phrase that is not standard, e.g., not that's wrong. If the phrase follows a NO, then it is in all probability a disagreement and not 01.
04	*Affirmation* (yes, right, ok) (as to truth value).
05	*Negation* (no, wrong) (as to truth value).
06	*Question* intended to obtain genuinely new information, which can also be an elaboration of the content of the previous utterance.
07	*Clarifying* query. If one partner did not immediately and fully understand the other's preceding utterance; can elicit clarification or mere acquiescence. "Mere acquiescence" is based upon the following communicational principle: You say something; I express how I understood your utterance; you will certainly correct me if I misunderstood you but you need not expressly agree if I understood you correctly. If you just proceed to the next topic, you provide evidence that the preceding topic is settled to your satisfaction.
09	*Testing* question; can be contingent or non-contingent. The mother obviously knows the answer and is only checking whether the child knows it/can express it too.
10	*Answer* to a question. Has to be a content answer, e.g., The dog is barking.
11	*Request* for permission or an expression of a wish/desire not directly requiring action by partner.
12	Specific request for action, or an utterance specifically *prescribing* how to act.
13	Verbal response indicating *compliance*/promise to comply. (You can only comply/refuse if a desire has been expressed. Need to be preceded by an 11, 12, or 14. Can also follow a 00, or the partner's YES/NO when asked about a specific wish.)

TABLE 3 (Cont.)

Computer code	Categories plus definitions
14	Verbal response indicating *refusal*/prohibition. (You only can comply/refuse if a desire has been expressed. Need to be preceded by an 11, 12, or 14. Can also follow a 00, or the partner's YES/NO when asked about a specific wish.)
15	Spontaneous *prohibition.*
16	*Interpretation:* Assignment of meaning if the preceding utterance is not clearly understood. The declarative sentence form differentiates this category from 07.
17	Signals *incomprehension:* often an attempt to elicit an improved formulation. WHAT? is usually coded as 17 and not as 07, since 07 presupposes evidence of at least partial comprehension.
18	Name or brief phrase used merely to *arouse* the attention of the partner. Vocatives are only coded 18 if they are the sole element of an utterance. Look, see, watch me are coded as 18 if conditions suggest a separate coding of these phrases.
20	*Repetitive* response without clear illocutionary force. Imitative utterances, but by far not all of them.
30	Mere *verbal play* (rhymes, rhythm, alliteration, songs)—no illocutionary force.
40	*Evaluative*/moral feedback: praise/scolding, conditioned reward/punishment for an act, can also be a verbal act. Praise for a verbal act can appear as well said, are you a clever girl, etc. Agreement as to truth value is 04.
99	Illocutionary force *ambiguous*/not clearly recognizable, or not subsumable under one of the above categories. Includes: Deixis, politeness forms, greetings, exclamations, and swearing.
00	*Uncodable.*

[a]The words marked in italic in Table 3 are employed in the Result section as key words to refer to the categories in question.

as they were formulated for the coders, the table can be treated as largely self-explanatory, and only a few remarks regarding the underlying rationale are needed. It is evident from Table 3 that the common classes of illocutionary force were repeatedly subdivided. This subdivision was undertaken in order that the categories might accord closer with the specific goals of the investigation and the specific population studied, i.e., the teaching and learning of a language and mother-child dyads, respectively. For example, 09, Testing Question, would be quite rare in normal conversations between adults; the frequency of 07, Clarifying Query, is a consequence of the immature language skills of the child, and 30, Mere Sound/Word Play, is also restricted to specific ages, or at least to very special situations. Since the illocutionary force pertains to the functional aspect of speech, all categories are defined on the basis of this criterion. That all categories are not equally finely subdivided is a consequence of the nature of interactions. The lower the frequency of occurrence of specific utterance types, the less reason to subdivide them.

(c) The code, encompassing phonetics, phonology, morphology, and syntax. This level is of great interest theoretically, since the code as modeled by the mother has to be one of the main sources of language learning by the child. It will nevertheless not be the main topic in the present report, which deals more with instructional methods and less with their content. Also in the present investigation, the range of the topics had to be restricted. Only transcripts and not the original tape-recordings of the verbal interactions were available, so that phonetic analyses were impossible. Since the transcriptions were made on the morphological level into typescript, even the phonological aspects of allomorph production could not be differentiated in many cases. Both the phonetic and phonological level will therefore be touched upon only exceptionally, when the data at hand make specific phenomena too impressive to be disregarded. For exhaustive analyses different types of data and different approaches are needed. The main emphasis will lie upon the syntactic and morphological aspects of the input. The syntactic aspect will be more intensively studied, since the pertinent phenomena are most ubiquitous in the model of the mother and since Eve, even at the earliest stages of the recording, showed some mastery of syntax in respect to word order. Attention will also be accorded to the 14 free and bound morphemes whose developmental history in Eve has been analyzed by Brown in several investigations. The present study will thereby serve as counterpart to these publications of Brown, since it presents the antecedent causes for the effects described by Brown.

The categories in Table 4 represent well-established grammatical concepts and need no explanation. What has to be explained is why they were chosen from the large variety of possible contents that need to be mastered in the course of language acquisition. For the first section, the 14 morphemes studied by Brown, the reason for their selection has already been given. For the selection of the syntactic aspects, the rationale can only be sketched out briefly. It is composed of partly practical and partly theoretical reasons. The practical reason underlying the choice of all categories was that the syntactic types in question had to appear frequently enough both in the speech of the mother and the child to provide reasonable chances to discover teaching-learning processes. The theoretical reason for the choice of the first two syntactic categories, the structures of full-verb sentences and the structures of the copula sentences, is explicated in a separate study (Moerk, 1979) in much more detail than would be possible here. In brief, it is postulated that English and most Indogermanic languages are based upon two basic syntactic frames: on the one hand the subject-verb-object frame and the subject-verb frame in the case of transitive and intransitive verbs; and an equational sentence frame, $X = y$, on the other hand. The former is seen as being cognitively derived from a Human-Action-Frame and the latter from an Object-and-Attribute Frame (Moerk, 1979). The equational sentence is encountered in

TABLE 4
Features of the Language Code That Were
Analyzed in Detail

(a) The 14 morphemes studied by Brown (1973):
The present progressive
on
in
Plural
The possessive (in contrast to Brown, who explored only the genitive case, the posses-
sive pronouns singular were included in the present analysis)
Past regular and irregular
Articles
The third person singular regular and irregular
The contractible and uncontractible copula
The contractible and uncontractible auxiliary.

(b) Syntactic aspects:
The structures of full-verb sentences
The structures of copula sentences
Interrogative sentences
The structures of the predicate in copula sentences
The structures of the subject noun phrase in full-verb sentences
The structures of the verb phrase in full-verb sentences
The structures of the object noun phrase(s) in full verb sentences (encompassing both di-
rect and indirect objects)
The structures of the prepositional phrases
Concord between the different constituents of a sentence (including concord between ele-
ments within constituents)
Name (Noun) - Pronoun equivalences
The types and structures of complex sentences

English in the form of the copula sentence; in other languages, and especially in child speech, the copula is however often omitted. Having specified the rationale for the two major sentence frames, little explanation for most of the other categories in Table 4 is needed. They represent the major sentence constituents and their relations to each other as in the case of Concord and Name (Noun) - Pronoun Equivalences. Two categories are added that record the modeling of optional transformations in Chomsky's sense, namely 'Interrogative Sentences' and 'Complex Sentences.' Both these types appear often enough in mother-child interactions, the first in full form and the second mostly in non-finite form, to make a search for cause-effect relationships meaningful. The study of "Complex Sentences" offers an additional interesting aspect: the more complex the sentence, the higher the danger that the child's language processing capacities might be overtaxed. A large number of complex sentences could therefore be an index of less-than-optimal maternal teaching strategies.

The above described three aspects of utterances, the message content, the interactional function, and the characteristics of the code, are quite generally focused upon in research. The setting, the goals, and the subjects of the study entail a fourth aspect, that of the instructional function or instructional potential of utterances. As was argued in the introductory section, the mother's input has of necessity also the function of making the structure of the code obvious to the child if she wants to assure effective communication between herself and her child. How the mother does this is of great theoretical and practical interest. Many investigators have specified some of these instructional techniques (R. Clark, 1974, 1977; Cross, 1975; Moerk, 1976 (a); Shatz, 1977). The present goal was to integrate many of these previous conceptualizations as far as they were pertinent to the aims of the analysis and as they were encountered in the verbal interactions of Eve and her mother. If conceptualizations were borrowed from other authors, the terms they employed to label their conceptualizations are employed too, in order to acknowledge the indebtedness to them. Often, however, conceptualizations had to be changed and adapted and the employment of new terms was then necessary. Whereas this broad indebtedness is acknowledged, it could not be attempted to trace the roots of all the categories employed to the variety of authors who established and developed them. In Table 5, the code numbers, the category labels which will be used in the Result section, and careful explanations and descriptions of the conceptualizations are given. These extensive descriptions, including coding advice, will not only make possible the independent evaluation of the codes employed but also their application by other investigators.

Since the explanations given were clear enough to the assistants who did most of the coding, it can be presumed that no further clarifications are needed here. Specific remarks as to the linguistic and psychological significance of the categories will be encountered throughout the Result section. Some discussion of the problems encountered in the use of those categories and of the ways they were dealt with is however needed. A consideration of the instructional techniques described in Table 5 suggests that the categories employed are not mutually exclusive. It was therefore attempted at first to code only "the most important category" for each utterance. This attempt soon came to nothing due to the diverging judgment of the coders as to what might be "most important." It was therefore decided to employ multiple coding of up to three instructional techniques per utterance. Six columns, cc 15 to 20, of the computer card were reserved for this purpose. In cases where more than three categories were recognized as being applicable to a single utterance, it was decided that the coders should arbitrarily eliminate all above the number of three. Since a single coder only rarely specified four or more categories for a single utterance, this loss of information was considered negligible and the arbitrary exclusion of some items did not seriously interfere with the reliability goal of at least 80% intercoder agreement. Considering the complexity of analysis and the almost certain incompleteness of the ana-

TABLE 5
The Categories Employed to Code the
Mother's Instructional Techniques

Computer code	Categories plus definitions
01	Identical and reduced imitation of linguistic elements. If only *I/you* are substituted for each other, or names and object labels are replaced by *he/she, it/that,* the imitation is coded as identical. This applies also to *my/your* substitution.
02	Expands child's utterance, which consists of 2 or more constituents (although this is not an absolute necessity). To code 02, the expansion has to consist of minor elements only, mostly functors. It mostly entails a corrective aspect and does only minimally alter the meaning; otherwise, code 07 applies.
03	Mere structural imitation. Frequently used structures such as the simple copula sentence and simple full verb sentences are normally not coded here. Look for rare forms: PPhs, Advs, Pass., Neg., wherein a causal influence of the preceding utterance is probable. 03 can be coded when only parts of the model are reflected in the syntax of the imitated utterance.
04	Imitation with instructive substitution of items. Include: pairs wherein singular and plural, Saxon Genitive, and the possessive pronoun (e.g., *Eve's - your*) are substituted for each other and all substitutions of pronouns in oblique cases (e.g., *me, him, her, us,* etc.).
05	Combinatory imitation: combines elements from two or more child utterances for own statement. If the elements were first produced by the child, it is a 05 even if the mother imitated one of the utterances of the child before.
06	Incorporates child's utterance, which is only a single constituent, into own, more-constituent message. (The item incorporated should be only minimally changed, but can involve minor contrasting correction; e.g., C. *No* - M. *Don't. . . .*)
07	Chaining or Coupling: Combines elements from partner's with own newly produced or repeated elements. (With occasional questions, look for chaining.)
08	Two-person sentence: A sentence fragment is uttered by the mother, which completes a preceding utterance of the child. E.g., C. He is working. M. At home. C. I see him. M. Yes, in the garden (meaning: You see him in the garden.)
09	Partial or full identity with partner's utterance; also, a repetition of own utterance. (A combination of 01, 02, 04 plus one of the 20-categories.)
10	Quotations: items from books, stories, or songs. A one-word title of a story will mostly not be coded as 10, as long as it does not obviously contain important linguistic information.
20	Repeats own statement (almost) identically. Has to be a content utterance, not *hm, yes,* etc. Meant as a technique; the goal is rehearsal, not just a repetition of a request that went unfulfilled. All major content elements have to remain the same, although their form can change, e.g., *eat - ate,* N - pronoun. The definition of identity is the same as for 01.
21	Completions. Successive constituent encoding in separate utterances or even turns, e.g., *Cromer busy. At home.* Uttered by the same person; can be

TABLE 5 (Cont.)

Computer code	Categories plus definitions
	typed on the same line, being merely separated by dots, e.g., *Anna make . . . tapioca.* As the example suggests, the dots should separate constituents to code 21. It should always be coded as two utterances; the code 21 is coded with the second utterance.
22	Build-up sequence of own utterance (if not done by partner before). Has to represent an addition of constituents or elements in the utterance, not just a replacement; but it can be accompanied by a deletion of other constituents. Normally not more than one full superordinate clause. Can contain a constituent-replacing clause, such as an object clause. (Addition of adverbial clauses = 58.)
23	Break-down sequence of own utterance (if not done by partner before, in which case it is a xx - 02 - 01 sequence). Has to represent the elimination of words or constituents.
24	Perseveration of specific morpheme or morpheme category, i.e., morpheme teaching (e.g., *did, -ed, -ing, n't, -s* Plural, etc.) despite changing content. Include: bound morphemes, auxiliaries, possessives, + "category" (all items of the same category even if different in form,e.g., all past tenses).
25	Replacement sequence: full or abbreviated syntactic structures. Either contentives (excluding auxiliaries) or meaning change. Has to be the same frame, and one constituent has to remain the same with each step. Replacement sequence corresponds to the "instructive substitution of items" as defined for 04, but now for same-speaker sequences. The differentiation of 01 from 04 corresponds to that of 20 from 25.
26	Replacement sequence of minor elements (particles of separable verbs, auxiliaries, determiners, prepositions) within the constituent (NP, VP, PPh). Frame variation is irrelevant. As in 25, the syntactic structure has to be manifest or to become more obvious in the course of the replacement sequence. This can be achieved by means of content similarity or obvious juxtaposition of structures.
27	Frame variation: repeats fully or partially the content; changes partially the syntactic structure. At least one element has to remain the same, and at least one of the elements has to change within the sentence frame; mostly it changes constituent function, (e.g., *You* was first subject and becomes an element in a PPh: *for you*) but sometimes there is only word-order change without constituent function change. Often but not exclusively from FV to copula sentence. Includes sequences of sentences with transitive and intransitive verbs if the structures are juxtaposed and their relationship is suggested through partial content similarity. Includes also questions with different syntax (word order, etc.) and same content.
28	Optional transformations: Only Declarative - Imperative - Question - Negation - Passive - Negative Question - Negative Passive - Question Passive - Indirect Question of Object Clauses, i.e., change in sentence type; the illocutionary force is irrelevant. Note: Single word utterances cannot be transformed! The transformational aspect has to stand out, so that it could be noticed by the child. This presupposes temporal proximity, obvious content similarities, or stylistic/structural juxtapositions.
29	Perseveration of new or rare vocabulary items. Mainly full verbs and nouns;

TABLE 5 (Cont.)

Computer code	Categories plus definitions
	can include modal auxiliaries. The goal is to register both intensive rehearsal and long-interval reinstatement. It applies therefore to massed items as well as to single repetitions within the hour sampled, if the item was new rare. It may often follow the intentional introduction of items which would have coded as 55, 56, or 57. The latter are then followed by one or more 29 codes.
40	Contrasting correction: The child says or comprehends (as shown through her nonverbal activities) something incorrectly; the mother corrects the incorrect element in her own utterance. To be differentiated from 02, which is an expanding correction. (E.g., C. *That's a cat.* M. *That's a dog.* C. *Papa goed.* M. *Papa went.* C. *Animal.* M. *Dog.*) Do not include corrections of pronunciation/enunciation.
41	Challenge: Challenges a verbalization of the child which was incorrect/less than optimal, mostly in question form, without correction. (E.g., *Is this a duck?* after child has labelled a hen *duck; You wented to school?* after child employed the incorrect past *wented* for *went;* or *Three mens?* in response to child's identical structure.)
50	Provides labels: Only one single content element, including *That is. . .* and *There. . .* sentences; as soon as there are two or more content elements, code 51, e.g., *Fraser's coffee.* Proper names well known to the child are not coded as 50.
51	Structural, syntactic mapping between linguistic expression and reality. Involves two or more content elements. The subject can be implied with single verbs and adjectives. There has to be some observable reality within the immediate experience which is being mapped. Code possession only if it is clearly visible/obviously known. Absence can be visible, e.g., *Half your dolls are missing.* Differentiate this category carefully from 71.
52	Parallels between linguistic expressions which are equivalent/have similar meaning and are not codable as 22, 23, 25, 26, 27, or 28. Planned as a "wastebasket" category; used if something is expressed twice and cannot fully be coded under another category. For example, the mother employs different syntactic constructions to express the same content, such as possession: have/Saxon Genitive/belong.
53	Asks for label (testing and regular questions). Includes: color labels, *What are you having for lunch? What are you cooking?*
54	Asks *What doing* question (testing and regular questions).
55	Feature elaboration: Develops a feature description out of a previous utterance, which often was labeling. Will mostly pertain to adjectives and adverbs and often have the illocutionary code 01. Does not include the possessive. We expect a stepwise development. First the object is given, next it is elaborated; if the elaboration is maintained, code as 29.
56	Dynamic elaboration: Develops a topic out of a previous utterance; often an action description of the object in question. Mainly finite verb forms. A technique used to smuggle in verb training. We expect a stepwise development here too as in 55.
57	Functional elaboration: Expands on uses/functions the item of discussion can be put to. Often non-finite verb phrases, e.g., *A bike is to ride on, Knives*

TABLE 5 (Cont.)

Computer code	Categories plus definitions
	are for cutting; but also We cut with knives and eat with forks. We expect a stepwise development here too as in 55.
58	Complex elaboration by means of adverbial clauses (time, place, cause, purpose, result, condition, concession). Also include adverbial clause equivalents, e.g., by putting. . . .
59	Asks a question requiring an adverbial clause as an answer.
60	Requests partner to repeat the preceding utterance, e.g., Can you say. . ., What? What did you say?
61	Item specification: Occasional question, incomplete sentence, or sometimes simply What, Who, Where, When, Whose. E.g., C. I lost. . . M. You lost what? or M. What? What did you lose? = 2 times 61. Also PPhs with item: You got it from where? or You are afraid of what?
71	Verbal encoding of internal states and feelings (no external evidence) in declarative form.
80	Feedback confirming that the preceding utterance was linguistically correct/ acceptable, e.g., good, yes, well said, good girl.
81	Feedback signifying that the preceding utterance was linguistically incorrect/not acceptable, e.g., no, wrong, No, not. . . But + question can have 81 function, e.g., Yes it's hot; But what is it?
99	Other. Includes: No recognized technique in content-bearing utterances plus all sound-patterns, deixis, and other specific techniques that could be recognized but are not in the key.
00	Uncodable. Includes vocatives, yes, no, ok, hi, but this code is mainly employed for gaps in the transcripts marked for inaudible utterance.

Note. The child's strategies were defined identically or equivalently, with only minor exceptions: Codes 80 and 81 were not employed for the child; code 40 is defined as "Selfcorrection;" code 02 represents "reduced and simplified imitation;" and code 01 stands therefore only for "identical imitation."

lytical system employed, a certain amount of information loss was inevitable.

A different and more serious reliability problem, however, arose. Given the complexity of the coding system and the much greater complexity of the linguistic medium that was being taught, it happened quite often, when each of the coders coded independently, that each chose one or a few codes for a specific utterance, that all of the chosen codes were correct in describing the maternal teaching techniques, but that the chosen codes were not identical. In such cases one or both the coders had not coded exhaustively all the techniques recognizable, though the codes of both were correct and complemented each other. Correctness in the code selection was therefore combined with differences in the codes selected and therefore with considerable unreliability. Even prolonged attempts by all involved to consistently attain exhaustiveness in coding all the instructional techniques, and thereby high reliability with independent coding, did not lead to satisfactory results. Attempts to reach exhaustiveness with a coding system encompassing 40 possible codes per utterance for maternal instructional techniques alone, whereby each utterance had to be related to at least a full page of the preceding text of the transcript and in the case of code 29 even to the entire hour of observation, proved too costly in information processing demands and therefore in coding time for each coder. Complete exhaustiveness could certainly not be guaranteed, even after the most serious attempts. It was therefore decided that at the present state of the art in the coding of maternal teaching techniques exhaustiveness was not attainable, and neither was high reliability in the strict sense, as this measure is normally computed. The reliability concept was therefore defined less ambitiously for the present study and pertains only to the correctness of the coding but not to its exhaustiveness. Procedurally, this meant that, when performing intercoder reliability checks, the second coder did not code the transcript independently but took the codes of the first coder and evaluated them on the basis of his/her own assessment of the transcripts. Judgements of incorrectness were defined as intercoder disagreements, whereas additional codes were discussed and—if agreed upon by both coders—were added to the original codes. The percentages of intercoder reliabilities reported pertain to this type of agreement/ disagreement. Since these percentages are at least in the eighties and often in the nineties, considerable assurance of the correctness of the coding exists, but these percentages do not imply that the coding was equally exhaustive.

With this major adjustment, the goal of high intercoder agreement was—almost—attained. One last problem arose in regard to category 29, Vocabulary Perseveration. Since no complete list of the vocabulary employed by Eve and her mother was available, the judgment as to what was a new or rare vocabulary item had to be made by the coders from their knowledge of the transcripts. There always appeared a few cases where the coders disagreed about the newness of a word and about whether it should be coded as 29 or not. Since after the introduction of new or rare words there followed mostly a period of intensive rehearsal and employment of the word in various syntactic frames, one contrast in judgment could lead to a considerable discrepancy in the percentage of agreement, when one coder had coded many 29s at every repetition of a specific word and the other coder had not coded a single 29 in regard to the same word. For reliability computations, it was therefore decided that disagreements in the code 29 would only be counted once in connection with each new or rare word and not whenever the word was repeated.

These were the reliability problems that could not be solved in accordance with the strictest criteria of the concept of reliability. Nevertheless it was considered more productive to attempt a rich and challenging analysis while acknowledging certain methodological problems than to produce a methodologically almost perfect but conceptually impoverished and practically sterile study. That there is much room for improvements is most obvious to the writer after he has struggled for over two years with the tasks of making such improvements.

Quantitative Analyses

(a) **Frequencies.** Three types of results will be discussed whose frequencies are of theoretical interest: instructional contents and the frequencies of their transmission; instructional techniques and the frequencies of their application; and interactional structures in their relative and absolute frequencies. Frequencies for individual samples, developmental trends in frequencies over the period under study, and frequencies for all 10 samples together will be reported. These input frequencies can then be compared with the speed, the age, and the level of mastery of specific linguistic items. Positive relationships between high frequencies of input and acceleration in acquisition can then suggest a causal influence of the input frequency.

(b) **Joint and transitional probabilities.** The interactional structures whose developmental trends are going to be ascertained can be described in a variety of ways. On the least complex level, joint probabilities or cooccurrences of two utterances in sequence, referred to as "pairs" or "doubles" subsequently, can be recorded. Four types of doubles are possible: Child - Mother, Mother - Child, Mother - Mother, and Child - Child sequences. For the present goals, the Child - Mother sequences are of greatest importance, since they demonstrate how the mother reacts to the utterances of the child which mostly if not always contain linguistic deficiencies. Mother - Mother sequences are generally extensions of Child - Mother sequences in that the mother produces two utterances in immediate succession after noticing a linguistic deficiency or encountering a conversational difficulty. They will therefore be studied in detail. Mother - Child sequences can offer suggestions as to the effectiveness of maternal interventions and are also relevant. Whereas Child - Child sequences provide evidence for language mastery strategies of the children, they do not pertain closely to the goals of the present study. Their discussion will therefore be delayed for further reports.

Joint probabilities signify only how probably, relative to all other possible doubles, two strategies/techniques cooccur in sequence, but they do not necessarily imply a tight structural sequential dependency. Only if the joint probability of a specific pair is considerably higher than would be expected from random cooccurrences, which implies a higher than randomly expected transitional probability, can such interactional structures be postulated. The relations between the indices can best be expressed in a formula:

$$p\,(i,j) = p(i) \cdot p\,(j/i)$$

whereby $p(i,j)$ is the joint probability, $p(i)$ the probability of the first item of the pair, and $p(j/i)$ the transitional probability that the second item of the pair follows the first one. An example might clarify the concepts and terms: Very young children might not yet have learned that real questions almost always require a verbal answer. They might provide verbal answers in only 50% of the instances questions are asked. The transitional probability of an answer following a question will therefore be .50. If, however, mothers ask many questions during early infancy, the joint probability of question - answer sequences might still be high in relation to the probabilities of the other possible pairs. In the course of development, children would learn about the necessity of answering questions, and the transitional probability of an answer following a question would increase and approach 1.00. If, however, during the same course of development mothers significantly decrease the frequency of their questions in relation to other types of verbal utterances, then the joint probability of question - answer pairs in relation to all other pairs of sequences could decline equally steeply as the transitional probability increases. Normally, the developmental trends of these two types of probabilities must be assumed to be quite independent. Challenging questions will therefore be encountered in the interpretation of the various quantitative indices and their trends.

It follows from the above discussion that transitional probabilities are the better indicators of conversational structure. But joint probabilities and the frequencies of cooccurrences are psychologically more interesting and meaningful. For even if the transitional probability of a pair would approach 1.00, i.e., certainty, but if the pair would almost never appear in normal conversations, little impact upon teaching and learning could be expected from the pair in question. To provide both an impression of the instructional importance and also of the conversational structure of specific interaction patterns, a combination of indices is desired. For the former, frequencies of cooccurrences, which are taken from the actual computer coding, will be given. For the latter, a value derived from the comparison of observed cooccurrences and expected cooccurrences will be provided. Expected cooccurrences are computed as the product of the separate probabilities of each member of the double, multiplied by the total number of doubles. To compare the two measures, one of the more commonly suggested indices is the binomial test z score (Bakeman, 1978). It is computed in accordance with the following formula:

$$z = (f_{obs.} - f_{exp.})\Big/\sqrt{f_i \cdot p_j (1 - p_j)}$$

Wherein f_{obs} is the observed frequency of cooccurrences

f_{exp} is the expected frequency of cooccurrences

f_i is the frequency of the first element of the pair

p_j is the probability of the second element of the pair

Since the denominator represents the variance of the differences between predicted and observed frequencies, the z score is a standardized index for comparing the differences between obtained and expected values. As N increases above 25, the binomial distribution approximates a normal distribution wherein a z score exceeding ± 1.96 would be significant at the .05 level or better. However, since the data do not consist of independent measures, no exact significance levels can be associated with the z scores. Though the z scores can be considered only as an index, the authors most versed in its application (Bakeman, 1978, Gottman & Bakeman, 1979) still recommend considering z scores above 2 as indicating sequential structure. In the Result section, only those patterns will be emphasized that obtained a z score considerably above the value 2.

Sequential cooccurrences of two interactional items are, however, quite incomplete descriptors for conversational processes. It is quite obvious that longer chains of utterances are produced in the discussion of even simple topics. For mother - child interactions, Moerk (1976a) found chains of five to six items as being quite common, and for interactions between married couples, Gottman, Markman, and Notarius (1977) found structures extending over six to seven items. Even longer sequences certainly have to be expected for individual topics. Completely to avoid consideration of longer sequences would therefore represent a distortion of the interactional phenomena encountered. In tackling these longer sequences, formidable obstacles arise, however. The first is that of descriptive sufficiency. In the present study with approximately 80 different categories, 40 of the mother and 38 of the child, the number of possible combinations of three elements is 80 to the third power, or 512,000. If sequences of five items are considered, the number of possible combinations surpasses three billion. To interpret such diversities would not only be cognitively impossible, it would also be ill-advised, since no sample size could be large enough to assure that each of these possible combinations could attain its real distribution.

Only preliminary attempts to solve these problems will be encountered in the present study. All occurring sequences of up to three categories were indeed counted with the help of a computer, and the more frequent ones will be presented and discussed in the Result section. Since the frequencies of single triples, even if derived from the total corpus of the ten samples analyzed, has of necessity to be low, another approach is employed too. Instructionally important strategies/techniques are selected as criteria, and it is explored which codes cooccur as the second and third members of the triplet. These items in third place can then be interpreted as being in a certain sense equivalent, since they share the privileges of cooccurrence with the preceding pair. Variations around this methodology of shared cooccurrences can then be performed. Lag sequential probabilities as developed by Sackett (1979) were considered for the analysis of longer sequences. Since the present study deals with around 80 categories, it was decided that the information to be obtained from this approach might not be very helpful to ascertain interactional structures. Further logical analyses of the possibilities inherent in lag sequential probabilities are, however, intended.

Having preliminarily dealt with the problem of describing at least triple sequences, labelled "triples" or "triplets" in the Result section, the more complex task of interpreting these sequences has to be faced. As soon as longer sequences of utterances are studied, it becomes obvious that a subsequent utterance is not or not only influenced by the one immediately preceding it, but more or equally by some preceding it two or three steps earlier. This is the problem of multiple influences that can mathematically be handled by higher order Markov chains. With such higher order Markov chain models, the combined and separate effects of several preceding variables upon a subsequent one can be analyzed. It will be seen in the Result section that this problem has been handled only by means of intuitive analyses based upon interactional and conversational principles and not yet by means of mathematical methods. Both lagged dependencies and multiple influences are certainly encountered in mother - child interactions, so that the challenges for further research are great indeed.

In the preceding sections, the applicability of conditional probability approaches and Markov models has been presumed. Before this approach is actually employed in much of the Result section, some theoretical weaknesses in the match between data and method have to be spelled out. It has been briefly mentioned that, mainly for triple sequences, the largest possible sample is required. The same applies, even if less urgently, for doubles. It would therefore be best to combine all 10 samples from the entire developmental period of Eve that was studied. On the other hand, it is a precondition for the computation of conditional probabilities and the employment of Markov models that the process is stationary, that is, that the probabilities do not change over the course of the period studied. Those two requirements cannot be fulfilled in the strict sense on the basis of the present data. To assure stationarity, samples from very brief developmental periods are preferable. Moerk (1974, 1975) and many other authors have, namely, shown that in the course of development the frequencies and relationships of many verbal interaction categories change. To increase the chance that the frequencies of pairs and triples attain their actual distributions, at least the ten samples that were computer coded have to be pooled. If one tries to discount the danger of lack of stationarity because the entire developmental period is quite short, around ten months only, it can be countered that Eve progressed very rapidly during this period in her linguistic skills and that pronounced developmental trends are found for individual categories and also for interactional pairs. Specific triple sequences attained such low frequencies that it is evident that those sequences cannot be expected to have attained their real distributions in the brief period of two hours of interactions which made up one sample. A description of trends for triples would therefore be unjustified; the data would mainly reflect random fluctuations.

This dilemma between too small a sample size for the attainment of the real distributions within individual samples and lack of stationarity across the developmental period could not be solved to one's complete satisfaction. It was therefore decided to provide three sets of data and to make thereby a careful comparison possible: (a) computations employing all the data from the ten samples were made, wherein the results are partly distorted by lack of stationarity; (b) values for the same indices are presented from individual samples where stationarity can be more confidently assumed but wherein deviations from the real distributions have to be expected due to small sample size; (c) results concerning the trends over samples are given so that an impression can be gained as to the deviation of the data from stationarity. An additional aspect of the data presentation that was necessitated by practical considerations alleviates somewhat the problems just discussed. Due to the large number of possible and actual pairs and triples, only those conversational structures appearing more frequently could be presented and discussed, and all the infrequently appearing ones, for which distortion through small sample size is more probable, had to be omitted. If clear patterns in frequently appearing items are observed over the developmental period, the confidence is enhanced that they represent real interactional and developmental dynamics. It will be seen in the Result section that, for the more frequent categories of interaction and for pairs of items considerable congruence exists between the data from single samples when compared with each other and with the results obtained from all ten samples together. This suggests that, notwithstanding methodological shortcomings and developmental trends, a considerable number of rather stable interaction structures have been discovered.

Having considered the methodological problems and the complexities of interpretation entailed by the reliance upon conditional probabilities and Markov models, it has to be justified why this approach was employed at all. The answer to this is its eminent appropriateness for the topics to be studied. Concerning the topic of illocutionary force, it is, e.g., of great interest what the probability or proportion of answers by the child is to the mother's questions. A high probability shows that the child has learned conversational rules. In the realm of strategies/techniques, it is of great interest to see, e.g., what the probabilities of maternal corrections are after diverse types of linguistic mistakes by the child. These results would give some insights into the controversial questions of maternal teaching intensity. For these and more complex questions, simple and lagged probabilities and higher order Markov chains are best fit to establish the quantitative indices from which answers can be derived.

RESULTS

Before the masses of results are presented, a set of data shall be introduced which can be of many uses. These are the ages and the MLU's of Eve's speech at the time the samples were collected. Foremost, the ready availability of these data will help the reader to interpret and evaluate intuitively many of the results. Second, the provision of these "independent variables," or better, "exogenus variables" in path analytic terminology—since the mother's input features are the main "independent variables" of interest—will allow other investigators to perform various cross-checks and meta-analyses. The wish for some additional analyses might immediately arise for many readers due to the fact that extreme selectivity in the data presentation had to be exerted. Of several possible ways to describe the results, only one could be chosen, in order to reduce the large amounts of data to be presented. For example, developmental trends are certainly of great psychological interest. They are also presented in many of the following tables. The question arose, however, whether to present these developmental trends on the basis of absolute frequencies or relative ones, i.e., percentages. Since the verbal interactions of mother and child became more intensive over the developmental period studied, that is the length of the transcripts increased considerably, most developmental trends based upon absolute frequencies would have been highly positive. Accompanying these increases in absolute frequencies was, however, often a quite steep decline in relative frequencies of certain interaction categories. Developmental trends based upon relative frequencies might therefore better represent changes in emphases than those based upon absolute frequencies. While relative frequencies might reflect emphases, absolute frequencies might depict learning opportunities for the child, and no clear-cut decision as to the psychological advantage in presenting either set of data could be made. A compromise was therefore chosen. For the individual samples and the totals, absolute frequencies are provided. The developmental trends were, however, computed on the basis of the relative frequencies, i.e., percentages. If for some reason developmental trends based upon absolute frequencies are desired by a reader, Table 6 gives data for the exogenous or independent variables and the data for the dependent variable are found in the tables. The correlations of interest can therefore easily be computed.

Little needs to be added to the data in Table 6. The close similarity in the trends represented by both sets of data is clearly evident. The Pearson Product-Moment correlation between them is .98. This fact will be of impor-

TABLE 6
Eve's Age in Months and MLU in Morphemes at the
Time the Samples were Collected

Independent variables	Sa 1	Sa 3	Sa 5	Sa 7	Sa 9	Sa 11	Sa 13	Sa 15	Sa 17	Sa 19
Age/months	18	19	20	21	22	23	24	25	26	27
MLU/morphemes	1.39	1.98	2.00	2.52	2.68	2.89	3.21	4.03	3.80	4.22

tance when an attempt is made to interpret some of the complex cases of suppression found in the Result section.

Conversational Themes and Functions

The structure and dynamics of themes. A first impression of the structure of the interactions can be gained from the analysis of the episodes and their boundaries. Table 7 contains the data from which some general patterns can be abstracted.

Since all the frequencies for each sample are derived from interactions lasting the same length of time, namely two hours, general trends over the developmental period are immediately visible: The intensity of the interactions increases quite sharply, as seen in the overall sum and the sums for child and mother separately. The pertinent correlations, based mostly upon percentages, with age, MLU, and the multiple R when the two exogenous variables are optimally combined, are given in the right-most column of this and all similar tables that follow. The steeply increasing trend in the Overall Total is in fascinating contrast to the contrasting trends in the Subtotals. Whereas the relative contribution of the child increases, the correlations range from the middle forties to the middle fifties, the relative contribution of the mother decreases almost to exactly the same degree. As a consequence of these contrasting trends, a higher degree of balance is attained between the contributions of mother and child. To evaluate the nature of the interactions, the frequencies of the specific episode codes are more informative. Code 3, New Topic, deserves closest attention. It signifies conversational leadership and stands in contrast to code 2, Unchanged Topic, which signifies conversational following. Comparing code 3 for child and mother, the clear leadership of the child in regard to the introduction of new episodes is obvious. Whereas the mother introduces a new topic less than 5 times per hour on the average, the child introduces new topics around 20 times. In contrast to this, the mother is much more prone than the child to continue with an old topic, code 2. The relationships between the frequencies of codes 3 and 2 reaches in some samples a proportion of 1:100 for the mother, whereas for the child, this relationship is as low as 1:4 and is mostly around 1:10. This contrast between mother and child is exacerbated when codes 4 and 5, Minor Change in the Topic and Return to a Preceding Topic, are added to the consideration. The child also leads in minor changes and in returns to preceding topics. The import of these differences for later analyses and for language acquisition generally can hardly be overemphasized: The mother, with few exceptions, deals with topics that are "old," i.e., they pertain to the preceding interactional context. The child therefore rarely encounters the task to abstract completely new content from the verbal input she receives. Since the mother employs mostly a theme proposed by the child and repeats it with minor and major linguistic varia-

TABLE 7
Frequencies of Utterances Defined as to Their
Episode-related Aspects

		The Child's Utterances										Total of 20 hrs	r[b] w/age	r w/MLU	Multiple R
Category	Code	Sa[a] 1	Sa 3	Sa 5	Sa 7	Sa 9	Sa 11	Sa 13	Sa 15	Sa 17	Sa 19				
No topic	1	5	4	20	7	2	0	9	30	18	19	114	.23	.27	.32
Same topic	2	127	148	390	332	277	185	337	611	387	463	3257	.72	.68	.73
New topic	3	37	24	41	48	43	32	41	43	40	27	376	-.63	-.70	.77
Minor change	4	8	15	7	9	4	6	14	14	10	5	92	-.55	-.52	55
Return to topic	5	19	18	11	37	23	10	6	31	15	17	186	-.57	-.50	.68
Uncodable	0	11	2	5	5	1	0	2	1	0	18	46	-.05	-.12	.36
Subtotal		207	211	474	438	350	233	409	730	470	549	4071	.49	.43	.55

[a]Two hours per sample were analyzed.
[b]All correlations were computed from the percentages of frequencies, in order to equalize for varying sample lengths.

TABLE 7 (Cont.)

The Mother's Utterances

Category	Code	Sa[a] 1	Sa 3	Sa 5	Sa 7	Sa 9	Sa 11	Sa 13	Sa 15	Sa 17	Sa 19	Total of 20 hrs	r^b w/age	r w/MLU	Multiple R
No topic	1	2	2	8	2	2	1	4	18	3	5	47	.19	.25	.40
Same topic	2	317	379	582	665	374	270	619	947	645	633	5431	-.39	-.34	.47
New topic	3	8	8	5	6	10	4	12	9	9	10	81	-.06	-.08	.11
Minor change	4	3	7	2	7	0	6	1	2	5	1	34	c		
Return to topic	5	4	9	5	10	4	6	7	10	11	3	69	-.50	-.40	.51
Uncodable	0	0	2	0	0	1	0	1	0	0	1	5	c		
Subtotal		334	407	602	690	391	287	644	986	673	653	5667	-.46	-.40	.53
Overall Total		541	618	1076	1128	741	520	1053	1716	1143	1202	9738	.61	.70	.80

[a]Two hours per sample were analyzed.
[b]All correlations were computed from the percentages of frequencies in order to equalize for varying sample lengths.
[c]There were too many cells with zero frequencies to compute meaningful correlation coefficients.

tions, Eve's information processing capacity can be mainly centered upon the mastery of the linguistic form. In terms of the differentiation made in the introductory section, mother-child interactions proceed mostly in the easiest form where the meaning of the message is well-known from previous linguistic context and from nonverbal situational cues. Since part of the form will be known too, the occasion for language learning is almost optimal.

The types and trends of conversational goals. Though only minimal attention can be given in this study to the illocutionary force of the interactions and the relationships between illocutionary force and instructional methodology, some data about the pragmatic aspects of the interactions shall be provided. The reasons for this are fourfold: First, being more familiar with the illocutionary aspects of conversations, the reader will get a better overall feeling for the character of the interactions. A knowledge of the illocutionary characteristics will also provide a basis for a better understanding of the results concerning instructional methodologies. Furthermore, possibilities for meta-analyses exist if the data are provided, and finally, the results are of great psychological interest in themselves. The categories of Illocutionary Force, their frequencies, and developmental trends in Eve's speech are presented in Table 8.

That declarative utterances, code 1, predominate is not unexpected on the basis of unsystematic observations and literature reports. The absolute frequencies of the categories 2 versus 3 and 4 versus 5 and their relationships shall be noted here, since they will soon be contrasted with the much larger number and the predominance of agreements in the mother's speech. Categories 7 and 9, the Clarifying Query and the Testing Question, respectively, were mainly designed for maternal speech and are consequently almost empty in the case of the child. Eve's clear increase in absolute and slight increase in relative frequencies of answers, code 10, is in some contrast to the mother's declining or stable frequencies of question asking, and suggests a gradual perfection of the question-answer pattern. Category 11, Requests for Permission, shows a steep decline in relative frequencies and probably reflects Eve's increasing volitional autonomy during her third year of life. This volitional autonomy is obviously not yet matched by motoric self-sufficiency, as the increasing requests for Action, code 12, suggest. Increasing volitional autonomy seems to be also reflected in categories 13 and 14, Verbal Compliance and Refusal, respectively. The correlational pattern in regard to category 14, Refusal, is of interest, since the contrast between the high multiple R and the much smaller zero-order correlations suggests a net suppression, in Cohen and Cohen's (1975) terminology, of the impact of one variable by that of the other. The partial correlations support this suggestion. They are for the age variable -.51 and for the MLU variable .57. It would be tempting to speculate that Eve, as she grows out of "the terrible twos," becomes more cooperative, but as she progresses in verbal skills, she learns to express her refusal more

TABLE 8

Frequencies of Categories of Illocutionary Force: Eve's Speech

Category	Code	Sa[a] 1	Sa 3	Sa 5	Sa 7	Sa 9	Sa 11	Sa 13	Sa 15	Sa 17	Sa 19	Total of 20 hrs	r[b] w/age	r w/MLU	Multiple R
Uncodable	0	13	7	24	44	17	2	9	1	6	22	145	-.48	-.50	.50
Declarative	1	64	68	146	141	161	85	149	272	141	171	1398	.25	.25	.26
Agreement	2	0	2	2	0	0	1	2	4	0	4	15	.20	.25	.32
Disagreement	3	2	2	0	1	1	0	0	7	3	10	26	.38	.42	.46
Affirmation	4	1	10	27	25	11	11	18	40	18	38	199	.58	.61	.62
Negation	5	2	0	9	23	7	10	6	13	12	10	92	.23	.20	.29
Question	6	15	6	33	24	13	11	56	77	74	60	369	.77	.72	.80
Clarifying	7	0	0	0	0	0	0	3	3	5	4	15	c		
Testing	9	0	0	0	0	0	0	1	1	0	3	5	c		
Answer	10	17	14	67	43	24	38	34	82	47	42	408	.15	.11	.24
Request	11	31	37	46	62	32	14	35	75	8	20	360	-.85	-.75	.97
Prescribing	12	9	23	11	16	19	28	14	31	45	57	253	.42	.37	.47
Compliance	13	1	0	1	6	2	5	7	14	9	8	53	.80	.77	.80
Refusal	14	2	3	4	4	2	2	0	15	6	9	47	.37	.47	.71
Prohibition	15	2	0	0	0	0	0	4	0	0	0	6	c		
Interpretation	16	0	0	0	0	0	1	0	0	0	0	1	c		
Incomprehension	17	0	0	0	2	1	0	21	31	22	6	83	.67	.68	.68
Calling attention	18	7	4	5	9	16	6	2	5	6	10	70	-.30	-.34	.39
Repetitive	20	28	23	70	16	26	6	31	8	14	8	230	-.77	-.82	.84
Verbal play	30	2	7	0	3	0	5	4	8	17	33	79	.61	.58	.61
Evaluative	40	0	0	0	0	0	0	0	0	0	0	0	c		
Ambiguous	99	11	5	29	19	18	8	13	42	33	34	212	.48	.44	.49

[a]Two hours per sample were analyzed.
[b]All correlations were computed from the percentages of frequencies in order to equalize for varying sample lengths.
[c]There were too many cells with zero frequencies to compute meaningful correlation coefficients.

29

often. But too little evidence exists to venture such speculative interpretations. From sample 13 on, it appears the child has mastered a new pragmatic skill to convey to the partner verbally that she didn't understand a preceding message, code 17, Incomprehension. Again, however, more detailed and qualitative analyses are needed. The trends in the last three defined categories, 18 plus 20 versus 30, can be described in one brief sentence: The more primitive types of utterances, i.e., codes 18 and 20, Attract Attention and Repetitive Response, decline, whereas the more complex one, code 30, Rhymes, Songs, increases. Moerk and Moerk (1979) have recently demonstrated the instructional potential that lies in such literary borrowings. Finally, one remark about an absent category may shed light on the quality of the interactions between Eve and her mother. During all the coding of the ten samples from Eve and her mother, the need for a category "Monologic Utterance" never became obvious. As soon as the investigator began, however, to code the interactions of Adam and his parents (Adam is also broadly known through Brown's research) the need for this category became immediately obvious. This suggests that interactional styles between dyads may profoundly differ. The pragmatic aspects of the mother's interactions are summarized in Table 9.

Table 9 is most meaningful when it is carefully compared and contrasted with Table 8. Comparing first categories 2 versus 3, 4 versus 5, and also 13 versus 14, while keeping the child's pertinent patterns in mind, it is seen that the maternal feedback is overwhelmingly positive. The proportions for the above-mentioned pairs is at least two to one and in the case of the simple *yes*, code 4, versus *no*, code 5, it is almost six to one. It will also be seen in later analyses that Eve's mother tries to avoid a response of *no* as much as possible. That the conclusion of previous researchers that the mother does not provide corrections is nevertheless incorrect will be demonstrated below.

The mother's declarative utterances, code 1, are far less predominant than the child's, and a pattern of suppression is again suggested by the correlations. The partial correlation for age is .31 and that for MLU is $-.29$. The almost identical values for the partial correlations, but with opposite sign in the case of suppression, that will be encountered quite consistently are due to the fact that the two independent variables, age and MLU, are almost perfectly related, $r = .98$. A considerable number of further instances of suppression is encountered in Table 9 and the partial correlations will be briefly presented, first that for age followed by that for MLU. For the code 0, Uncodable, they are: .28 and $-.32$; for code 2, Agreement, they are: $-.27$ and .24; for code 5, Negation *no*, .52 and $-.42$; for code 12, Request for Action, $-.44$ and .39; for code 13, Compliance, $-.54$ and .49; for code 14, Refusal/Prohibition, they are: $-.54$ and .43; and, finally, for code 40, Evaluative/Moral Feedback, they are $-.28$ and .31. No attempt will be made to interpret all those instances where the partial correlations with age and

TABLE 9

Frequencies of Categories of Illocutionary Force: The Mother's Speech

Category	Code	Sa[a] 1	Sa 3	Sa 5	Sa 7	Sa 9	Sa 11	Sa 13	Sa 15	Sa 17	Sa 19	Total of 20 hrs	r^b w/age	r w/MLU	Multiple R
Uncodable	0	1	2	2	2	2	1	2	1	4	1	18	-.16	-.22	.38
Declarative	1	44	84	91	101	78	58	170	135	143	106	1010	.12	.06	.31
Agreement	2	33	30	72	43	30	20	39	110	60	57	494	-.19	-.14	.30
Disagreement	3	13	3	16	35	19	17	29	54	37	37	260	.57	.55	.57
Affirmation	4	28	44	68	56	49	24	47	80	53	59	508	-.60	-.57	.62
Negation	5	4	0	7	5	12	10	9	15	16	10	88	.44	.35	.63
Question	6	40	34	60	64	31	22	52	79	53	72	507	-.49	-.49	.49
Clarifying	7	33	20	39	73	46	32	45	95	52	45	480	-.13	-.12	.13
Testing	9	17	8	64	40	3	28	20	79	26	28	313	-.07	-.06	.08
Answer	10	12	4	25	11	11	9	41	42	30	25	210	.46	.39	.56
Request	11	0	1	0	1	0	0	1	4	2	5	14	.64	.69	.73
Prescribing	12	27	59	49	76	30	20	58	89	70	54	532	-.32	-.24	.52
Compliance	13	23	42	27	58	20	25	25	71	41	47	379	-.33	-.23	.57
Refusal	14	15	23	17	46	21	1	22	28	3	18	194	-.62	-.54	.74
Prohibition	15	3	14	4	5	1	2	12	3	17	7	68	-.11	-.11	.11
Interpretation	16	12	7	2	12	1	1	8	8	3	17	71	-.33	-.32	.34
Incomprehension	17	22	7	16	23	16	3	12	13	9	11	132	-.68	-.70	.70
Calling attention	18	1	6	3	6	1	4	2	3	8	3	37	-.14	-.12	.16
Repetitive	20	1	1	1	8	1	2	3	6	5	13	41	.60	.61	.61
Verbal play	30	0	0	3	0	0	0	0	3	1	0	7	c		
Evaluative	40	2	11	11	9	2	3	22	23	9	9	101	.09	.15	.36
Ambiguous	99	3	7	25	16	17	5	25	44	31	29	202	.73	.73	.73

[a]Two hours per sample were analyzed.
[b]All correlations were computed from the percentages of frequencies in order to equalize for varying sample lengths.
[c]There were too many cells with zero frequencies to compute meaningful correlation coefficients.

31

MLU have the opposite sign, since such interpretations would be too speculative and premature, though the dynamics suggested by these patterns are
fascinating indeed.

In contrast, brief interpretations of the less complex patterns in Table 9,
where both independent variables have almost the same correlation with the
dependent ones, will be attempted. The results suggests that a differentiation
of questions into three distinct sets was fruitful, since each set exhibits a different developmental pattern. Only real questions show a clearly decreasing
trend in relative frequencies, whereas the clarifying query and the testing
question are stable as to percentages and increase in absolute frequencies.
The average of approximately one testing question per two minutes of interactions, wherein the mother checks whether the child masters a specific item
of linguistic knowledge, belies the assertion of many authors that mothers
generally are unaware that they teach language. The instructional sophistication obvious in later tables will also suggest at least a partial awareness, at
least in the case of Eve's mother. To assess all the instances in which the
mother had difficulties in fully comprehending Eve's messages, categories 16
and 17, Interpretation and Signals Lack of Understanding, have to be combined with category 7, Clarifying Query. Categories 16 and 17 are felt to indicate simpler interactional approaches, and their correlation patterns are also
somewhat different from that of code 7. The clear increase in answers on the
part of the mother, code 10, does nevertheless not fully match the increase in
the child's questions in Table 8, code 6. It reflects it only partly, since questions can be answered with compliance/refusal, codes 13/14, with affirmation/
negation, codes 04/05, and in a number of other ways. The relative decrease
in category 12, Request for Action, would be in accord with the above suggested interpretation of an increasing volitional independence of the child. It
might be of considerable interest that, in all the three categories dealing with
very practical behavioral matters, codes 12, 13, 14, i.e., Request for Action,
Compliance, Refusal/Prohibition, the negative partial correlations ($-.44$,
$-.54$, $-.54$) appear in relation to the age variable, whereas the partial correlations with MLU are throughout positive and quite high (.39, .49, and .43, in
the numerical order of the codes.) The frequent zero values for category 30,
Rhymes, Songs, are partially in contrast to the results obtained for the child,
and they are therefore surprising, since the child obviously learned and knew
several of these literary items. Whether Eve acquired them from other persons in her surroundings, or whether the mother's omission of these items
during the observation sessions represents her adjustment to the recording
situation, cannot be evaluated on the basis of the transcripts available.
Finally, it may be worthwhile noting that, in regard to code 40, Evaluative/
Moral Feedback, the partial correlations suggest a negative trend with age (r
$= -.28$) and a positive trend with MLU ($r = .31$). This pattern fits well to
those for codes 13, 14, and 15 and they all suggest that pragmatic aspects are

handled in this Harvard-student family on the verbal level as soon as the developing verbal skills of the child permit, even if those types of feedback decline in importance with the age of the child.

Instructional Content

In contrast to the preceding section, which was intended to reflect the theme-related structures and dynamics of the interactions, the following section shall almost exclusively be concerned with maternal language teaching and the child's reactions to it. To follow a trend from the easy to the more difficult topics, that is, from the better known to the more unknown areas of research, some aspects pertaining to the content of maternal instruction will be outlined first.

Input and acquisition of selected morphemes. Brown (1973) has summarized almost ten years of research of his group at Harvard and has expanded it in describing the acquisition by Eve of 14 morphemes and by suggesting possible variables that influence the speed of this acquisition. In doing this, he drew theoretically important conclusions that have been often—and quite often uncritically—quoted. He has concluded that minimal or no evidence exists that input frequency could be an important variable, and opted for "semantic complexity" as the major explanatory independent variable. Moerk (1980) has already dealt with the summary rejection of the effects of input frequency and has demonstrated that at least a very cautionary approach is advised, since clear evidence exists that input frequency might be of profound significance. He has also suggested that multiple variables might have to be considered in order to explain the acquisition process. This latter suggestion will be explored in somewhat more detail in the following three tables dealing with the 14 morphemes Brown analyzed. A brief synopsis of the input and acquisition of some possessive pronouns is added.

In Table 10, the frequency of maternal input and of Eve's use of some of Brown's 14 morphemes are presented. The morphemes selected are acoustically quite distinct, consisting either of a separate word, a word-final syllable with a stress-bearing vowel in it, or at least a quite noticeable change in the ending of a word, i.e., the regular past tense. This last case is, however, transitional in regard to acoustic distinctiveness. Within the table, the morphemes are arranged in a rank order according to their approximate input frequencies. The effect of input frequency appears quite clear if the frequency in Eve's use is considered as dependent variable. If more microscopic analyses were possible at the present, input effects could be shown even more clearly, as in the two lone appearances of the regular past in hour 3 of sample 2. Both were almost immediate repetitions by Eve of a maternal model. The appearance of the first two *in's* in hour 1, sample 5, follows the same principle. The first *in box* succeeds three immediately preceding models of *in the box*, and

TABLE 10
The Morphemes Analyzed by Brown in Input
and Productive Use

Morpheme Person		Acoustically distinct morphemes				
		Sample 1	Sample 2	Sample 3	Sample 4	Sample 5
Articles	M[a]	50b,57,62,16	85,50,68	41,52,37,39	103,127	93,50,56
		9,7,27,11	19,11,18	4,28,21,25	2,3,14	12,19,13
Present progressive		12,9,19,3	4,11,12	8,9,6,10	3,27	11,30,7
	E	,2,2,0	2,0,2	1,2,0,1	,6	5,16,7
Genitive case	M	8,10,20,4	3,2,9	,6,3,3	6,26	8,8,1
	E	7,5,8,3	2/3c,1,9	/1,3/1,3/1,4	12/2,1½	21,8,1
on	M	7,14,9,1	7,10,4	4,12,9,7	25,17	17,9,3
	E	0,0,2,0	1,0,1	,1,1,1	1,0	2,0,3
in	M	6,9,7,3	7,1,8	2,6,1,8	6,19	26,12,3
	E	0,0,0,0	0,0,0	0,0,0,0	0,0	2,0,0
Past regular	M	1,1,0,2	3,0,4	2,2,1,2	1,5	1,5,1
	E	0,0,0,0	0,0,2d	0,0,0,0	0,0	0,0,0

[a]M = maternal input;   E = Eve's productive use
[b]The commas separate the sums encountered during single hours within the sample. The various samples did not encompass the same numbers of hours.
[c]The slant separates the noun-noun constructions without the genitive morpheme *'s* on the left from those with *'s* on the right. All were employed to convey the meaning of possession. If no slant is employed, no constructions with the *'s* were encountered.
[d]The two instances of *spilled* were uttered by the child in immediate and briefly delayed imitation of a maternal model, respectively. They are therefore certainly a function of the input.

the next instance in the form of *in the toy box* follows immediately two maternal models: *Is it in the toy box?* and *Well, we'll see if it's in the toy box. In* is then employed three times by Eve in sample 6, and from sample 7 on it is employed several times in every hour of recording. The less frequent past regular is later employed in sample 7, three times in immediate succession, applied to a single word *pull* and seemingly in direct imitation of a sentence read to Eve. It is not used with any regularity before sample 9. Whereas input frequency appears to be the most important causal variable in Table 10, it might not be the only one. Though the Present Progressive is modeled more often than the Genitive Case, its regular use by Eve considerably postdates that of the noun-noun combinations expressing possessive relations. Whether the reason lies in the difference in acoustic distinctiveness or in the contrast between the addition of an entire word (in the case of the Genitive Case) as compared to a mere ending, the −ing of the Present Progressive, cannot be decided from the data in Table 10. Support for the distinctiveness-hypothesis could be derived from Eve's constructions approximating the Genetive Case. The Genitive Case consists obviously of two morphological phenomena: The noun-noun combination, and the s of the Genitive Case specifically. Eve very early masters the acoustically distinct phenomenon of combining two nouns to express possession, but she neglects throughout most of the first five samples to add the acoustically indistinct s. Finally, the Past Regular is not only modeled rarely by the mother but is also acoustically less distinct than most of the preceding morphemes. Its developmental history approximates therefore more closely that of the second group of Brown's morphemes, which are throughout acoustically quite indistinct.

TABLE 11
The Morphemes Analyzed by Brown in Input
and Productive Use

Acoustically weak morphemes					
Morpheme Person		Sample 1	Sample 2	Sample 3	Sample 4	Sample 5
Contr. copula	M[a]	40[b],40,87,25	51,51,61	48,41,30,49	75,81	75,57,52
	E	0,0,0,0	0,0,0	0,0,0,0	0,0	0,0,0
Uncontr. copula	M	13,27,43,9	30,17,31	35,28,21,13	29,44	27,41,21
	E	0,0,0,0	0,0,0	0,0,0,0	0,0	0,0,0
Contr. aux.	M	20,10,13,11	26,16,14	24,24,15,27	40,45	14,7,4
	E	0,0,0,0	0,0,0	0,0,0,0	0,0	0,0,0
Uncontr. aux.	M	5,6,18,19	42,24,38	21,26,20,25	47,43	7,17,9
	E	0,0,0,0	0,0,0	0,0,0,0	0,0	0,0,0
Plur. reg.	M	8,8,3,2	18,9,7	1,3,3,4	24,18	11,18,5
	E	0,0,0,0	1,0,0	0,0,0,0	1,1	1,3,2
3rd Pers. singular	M	0,4,0,0	3,0,4	4,0,0,1	1,0	3,0,8
	E	0,0,0,0	0,0,0	0,0,0,0	0,0	0,0,0

[a]M = maternal input; E = Eve's productive use
[b]The commas separate the sums encountered during single hours within the sample. The various samples did not encompass the same numbers of hours.

The common feature of all the morphemes in Table 11 is that they consist of an acoustically weak *s* allomorph which is at best combined with a very weakly stressed vowel preceding it. All these morphemes also have in common that in spite of input frequencies that match or surpass many of those in Table 10, none of them is employed with any consistency by Eve in these early samples. The contrast between the Tables 10 and 11 strongly suggests that the variable of acoustic distinctiveness is primarily responsible for the order of acquisition of the first minor morphemes. Brown (1973, p. 271 *et passim*) reports that the uncontractible forms of the copula and auxiliary are generally acquired before the contractible forms. Since, in the latter, the vowels have been deleted and the morphemes are therefore less distinct acoustically, this report of Brown's supports the presented hypothesis. Of all the morphemes in Table 11, the regular plural stands out, since it is employed by Eve in samples 4 and 5, as well as once in sample 2. The transcripts show that samples 4 and 5 do not yet represent Eve's transition to the regular use of the plural morpheme. It is employed with some regularity only from sample 10 on. But its early appearance requires some consideration.

One distinction between the plural and the other morphemes in Table 11 is semantic: the plural morpheme often carries non-redundant meaning, whereas the other morphemes are mainly grammatical markers and are semantically redundant. A semantic factor might therefore affect the early appearance of the plural −*s*. Detailed analyses of the transcripts show the following: In sample 2, it seems to be a case of transcription error. The transcript contains in parentheses the words *Woods or bird* as Eve's response to a question about a book. Eve never employs the word *or* during this early period, nor do the words *woods* and *bird* seem to be in her repertoire. Since the parentheses indicate that the tape signal was weak and barely audible, this instance of the plural can confidently be discounted. In sample 4, *blocks* follows immediately after a maternal model; it is a common vocabulary item in Eve's repertoire and the incidence seems therefore genuine. Later on, the −*s* of *nuts* is put within double parentheses in the transcript, suggesting near inaudibility, so that the genuineness of the instance has to be doubted. In sample 5, the first item, *blocks* was again indistinctly audible and is therefore suspect, although it might easily be genuine. *Christmas tree cookies* and *these pages* seem to have been clearly audible; both follow immediately after a maternal model and are probably genuine. *Bouillon cubes* was first uttered by Eve without the plural −*s* but was then improved upon by adding the −*s* immediately after two maternal models containing the −*s*. Finally, Eve imitates her mother's *I'm icing the cookies* with *Ice the cookies*. From these phenomena, it must be concluded that the immediately preceding input presented the predominant cause for those precocious appearances of the plural −*s*. Input frequency is probably involved in the case of *cookies, bouillon cubes,* and *blocks*, since they were often talked about in the family. Due to the nature of the data, no evidence exists for a role of semantic factors.

An almost ideal opportunity to disentangle semantic and frequency factors is provided by the possessive pronouns. Semantically, all of them are similar in referring to a possessor, though *my* and *your* (sing.) should be more difficult semantically, since their referents change during the dialogue whereas the referents of *his* and *her* do not change so systematically. *My* and *your* (sing.) are, however, modeled much more frequently in the input than *his* and *her*. Since possessive pronouns in the plural, as well as *its*, were extremely rare in the input, they are not discussed. Pertinent frequency data on the other pronouns in input and Eve's use are presented in Table 12.

TABLE 12
Maternal Input and Eve's Use of the Possessive Pronouns Singular

Morpheme Person		Sa 1	Sa 2	Sa 3	Sa 4	Sa 5	Sa 6	Sa 7	Sa 8	Sa 9	Sa 10	Sa 11
my	M	3	1	9	10	10	7	8	8	4	0	2
	E	5[a]	0	3	3	5	9	16	3	7	35	47
your	M	43	76	64	46	30	21	48	39	26	22	10
	E	0	0	0	0	0	0	0	0	0	0	10[b]
his	M	7	0	7	3	4	2	2	9	5	3	3
	E	0	0	0	0	0	0	0	0	0	0	0
her	M	4	2	1	0	1	1	10	7	1	0	1
	E	0	0	0	0	0	0	0	0	0	0	0

[a] Only semantically correct instances were counted. There were rare instances in which Eve seemed to employ *my* as a subject which were not included. Since Eve confused *my* and *mine* until sample 11 and often employed both almost exchangeably, both *my* and *mine* were counted due to their semantic and phonetic similarity.

[b] Only semantically adequate uses were counted again. This excluded the use of two *you's* with the meaning *her*, but included one morphologically correct use of *your*, five instances of *you* + noun with clear possessive meaning, and four *yours* with possessive meaning.

Table 12 presents a quite captivating picture. It demonstrates conclusively that semantic complexity is not a factor in the acquisition order of these pronouns. Otherwise *my* and *your* should be acquired last. But neither is frequency the only or even the most dominant factor. Certainly the two least frequent pronouns, *his* and *her*, are not employed even a single time by Eve up to sample 11. But the most frequently modeled pronoun, *your*, makes its appearance in Eve's speech only in sample 11, and even there only once completely correctly as *your*. In contrast, *my*, the second most frequently modeled possessive pronoun, appears earliest and most consistently. Quite evidently a combination of a frequency factor and a factor which K. Buhler (1934) labeled *Sprachnot* (need for language), or maybe better a parsimony factor such as Zipff's (1949) "principle of least effort" come into play. Eve shows, namely, in her noun-noun combinations that she has mastered all four conceptualizations involving the different personal possessors, and she employs these noun-noun combinations not infrequently in most of her samples. Only the possessive reference to herself is, however, so important for her that it is referred to very often and it is referred to in the most parsimonious manner.

In addition to the above analyses, Moerk (1980) presented further and stronger evidence of input frequency effects for all three of Brown's subjects, and he (Moerk, 1977a; Moerk et al., 1979) also provided suggestive data on the immediate and progressive impact of maternal models upon the imitations of the child. Several other authors (Bloom, Hood, & Lightbown, 1974; Clark, 1977; Forner, 1977; Savic, 1975; Whitehurst, 1977) have recently reported similar findings. It appears necessary, therefore, to study the question of input frequency from a broader perspective. This is done beginning with Table 13.

Input frequencies of selected syntactic items. Since language entails many diverse aspects, the question which of them to select for study arises. Probably more important than the acquisition of some bound and minor free morphemes, and certainly developmentally more primary, is the child's developing mastery of the major sentence frames and some of the most common transformational derivations. Table 13 will focus upon the input in regard to the two major frames of Full-Verb and Copula Sentence and the very commonly encountered questions. The fourth category in Table 13, Complex Sentence, is still very undifferentiated and is considered mainly as an overall index as to how much the mother taxes the linguistic capacity of her child. It includes at present coordination and subordination of clauses, but also infinitive and participial constructions and even the rare cases of multiple subjects and objects. Multiple adverbials were not employed as an indication to code sentences containing them as "complex."

Table 13 and the following tables contain not only data as to the observed frequencies but also estimated frequencies. The latter need some introductory qualifications. It is quite certain that the recording sessions do not represent a random sample of all the normal daily activities of the child. The verbal interactions during the recording sessions might therefore not provide a random sample of mother-child communication either. It is probable that, during the prearranged recording sessions, the mother of Eve interacted more intensively with her than she would during the normal course of the day. Since no research seems to exist comparing frequencies during arranged recording sessions with input frequencies during day-to-day interactions, the danger exists of overestimating the total input frequencies per day, week, or month when the basis for the estimate is the arranged recording session. This danger is counteracted by two methodological aspects: first, observer input was not counted, so that the reported frequencies per sample are somewhat lower than those actually recorded in the transcripts; second, in estimating frequencies per day, the averages per hour were multiplied only by 10,

TABLE 13

Observed Hourly and Estimated Frequencies with which Some Major Sentence Frames were Modeled for Eve

Type	Sa 1 Hr 1	Sa 3 Hr 1	Sa 5 Hr 1	Sa 7 Hr 1	Sa 9 Hr 1	Sa 11 Hr 1	Sa 13 Hr 1	Sa 15 Hr 1	Sa 17 Hr 3	Sa 19 Hr 1	Aver/ Hr	Est/ day	Est/ week	Est / month
S-V-(O)[a]	100	85	87	167	128	83	154	249	181	180	141	1414	9898	42.420
Copula[a] sentence	40	40	82	76	34	36	66	95	64	91	62	624	4368	18.720
Question	65	35	61	80	51	42	33	121	88	71	65	647	4529	19.410
Complex sentence	17	15	22	29	23	16	44	65	58	54	34	343	2401	10.290

[a] In all modalities, including questions.

39

though it is obvious that the waking day of a two- to three-year-old child is longer than 10 hours. Although an attempt was made to balance error sources, the provided estimates represent certainly only preliminary approximations, and a considerable error range has to be presumed. The estimates can not be generalized to the population of all mother-child dyads, but apply only to the population of verbal input provided to Eve. In spite of these error risks, it was considered valuable to present estimates of the probable input frequencies, since this has never been done to the knowledge of the writer and since the input factor is so commonly underestimated or even simply discounted as unimportant.

Table 13 does not need to be discussed in detail, since it seems quite evident that input frequencies of up to 100 per hour or even higher, and up to 40,000 per month, could not easily leave the child uninfluenced. It needs perhaps to be reemphasized that the child responded to almost all of this verbal input adequately, thereby demonstrating that she had analyzed it and absorbed the meaning of the messages. Considering the considerable prevalence of the full-verb sentence over the copula sentence in the mother's speech, it is of some interest that Eve's speech as described in Brown (1973, esp. Table 17 and Table 22) shows a similar preponderance of the full-verb sentence. Since pragmatic/functional variables certainly are involved in the choice of sentence type, the coincidence of the two frequencies certainly shall not be overinterpreted. Brown has shown that questions appear with their clear illocutionary intent and even in their grammatical form—even if a simplified one—during the earliest stages of Eve's language development, but develop fully only in her Stage III, that is towards the end of the observation period. These acquisition facts appear to accord well with the input evidence presented in Table 13. Finally, it is obvious that all children including Eve employ complex sentences quite late, which accords with the low input frequencies. But the category is still too undifferentiated to establish close cause-effect relationships between input frequencies and acquisition.

After the overall sentence frames have been studied, their constituents need to be considered. In Table 14 the observed and estimated frequencies of these various sentence constituents in the input provided by Eve's mother are presented.

Besides the obvious intensity of the input, a few specific phenomena have to be singled out for discussion. It has been generally reported that the subject noun phrase in child speech is very simple for a long time and contains mainly one element only. Looking at the input provided by the mother, this phenomenon might be easily explainable. Two-or-more-element subject-noun-phrases in the maternal input are extremely rare. Equally interesting is the fact that neither in child language output nor in Eve's mother's input does there exist a similar discrepancy in the object-noun phrase between one-element and two-and-more-element constructions. These overall and simple

TABLE 14

Observed Hourly and Estimated Frequencies with which Major Constituents
of the Full-verb Sentence were Modeled for Eve

	Type	Sa 1 Hr 1	Sa 3 Hr 1	Sa 5 Hr 1	Sa 7 Hr 1	Sa 9 Hr 1	Sa 11 Hr 1	Sa 13 Hr 1	Sa 15 Hr 1	Sa 17 Hr 3	Sa 19 Hr 1	Aver/ Hr	Est/ day	Est/ week	Est/ month
SNP	1 element	77	76	67	122	97	74	130	188	124	149	110	1104	7728	33120
	≥ 2 elements	9	0	5	4	4	1	2	6	7	1	4	39	273	1170
Full Verb Phrase	Only Full Verb	45	55	45	87	69	41	68	101	78	71	66	660	4620	19800
	Full Verb + Aux.	54	40	48	79	58	39	93	139	108	113	77	771	5397	23130
ONP	1 element	19	30	26	56	53	31	57	78	68	55	47	473	3311	14190
	≥ 2 elements	46	26	32	69	45	34	62	70	59	51	49	494	3458	14820
Adverb.	PPh	35	29	80	60	42	35	52	95	79	57	56	564	3948	16920
	Adverbs	9	39	37	56	45	32	37	26	67	42	39	390	2730	11700

41

parallels in maternal and child frequencies, however, no longer hold in the case of the verb-phrase. Though the mother employs somewhat more frequently full verbs plus auxiliaries in her verb phrase, children are generally found to begin with single verbs in the verb phrase position. Semantic/syntactical complexity seems to be the most probable cause for this discrepancy, though finer analyses would be needed to demonstrate it. It is, however, also a well-known fact that children begin quite early to employ semi-catenative auxiliaries such as *gonna, wanna, hafta*. Qualitative analyses of the transcripts that cannot be presented here strongly suggest that cause-effect relationships between input frequency and immediacy and employment by the child could be demonstrated in this case too. Although the developmental history of adverbials in Eve's speech has not yet been explored in detail, the overall impression gained from the transcripts suggests that it accords fully with the input frequencies shown in Table 14. That is, prepositional phrases are employed earlier and more generally than adverbs.

Table 15 presents a few data about phenomena that tie sentence constituents together, either strictly within the clause as in Concord or both within and across clauses as in Name/Noun-Pronoun Equivalence. Concord, mainly in person and number, was only counted in those cases where specific morphemes are supplied to express that concord, as in *I am* versus *They are*, but not when no specific morpheme was required to signify it, as in *I go* versus *You go*. The input frequencies are relatively low and, as was indicated above relying upon Brown's analyses of morpheme acquisition, the child's mastery is established late too. Aspects of acoustic indefiniteness and semantic redundancy are, however, involved in these types of grammatical constructions, so that a univariate causal explanation would probably be incorrect.

If input had not been so neglected factually during the last decades and so downgraded theoretically, the preceding section would have mainly belabored the obvious. Obvious, at least, as far as two thousand years of recorded experience with human learning are concerned, beginning with the Greek and Roman schools of rhetoric. Whereas only the obvious might have been reaffirmed, the psychological implications of these findings might not be so obvious. The findings as to the predominant or almost exclusive importance of acoustic distinctiveness and frequency of the input—at least during the early stages analyzed here—implicate mainly the sensory systems and a simple storage system in the child. The often emphasized cognitive capacities could in contrast almost be discounted in the explanation of the results presented above. These implications are a shock for the writer and probably even more for the *Zeitgeist*—and they shouldn't be. Every aware second-language teacher and learner could have suggested these rules: The acoustic signal has to be as distinct as possible to stand out from the stream of sounds, and thereafter it is rehearsal and rehearsal and rehearsal, before the tool, i.e., the linguistic item, can be used and can be used efficiently.

TABLE 15

Observed Hourly and Estimated Frequencies with which the Concord
Between Sentence Constituents was Modeled for Eve

Type	Sa 1 Hr 1	Sa 3 Hr 1	Sa 5 Hr 1	Sa 7 Hr 1	Sa 9 Hr 1	Sa 11 Hr 1	Sa 13 Hr 1	Sa 15 Hr 1	Sa 17 Hr 3	Sa 19 Hr 1	Aver/ Hr	Est/ day	Est/ week	Est/ month
Concord within clause	27	23	35	67	34	32	43	48	29	62	40	400	2800	12000
Name/noun-pronoun equivalence[a]	21	19	38	26	15	17	28	28	22	28	24	242	1694	7260

[a] Mostly across clauses.

43

But just to emphasize the importance of clarity and frequency of the input language for acquisition would be a very simplistic inference. Those two features are essential prerequisites but generally not sufficient conditions. Second-language teachers and middle class mothers have developed a wide variety of additional techniques to further language learning. The following main sections of this study will deal with these more advanced techniques.

Instructional Form

Frequencies of single techniques. In the description of the instructional form in maternal language teaching, relatively new and largely uncharted territory is encountered. Concern for maternal language input has only been demonstrated since around 1969, with the studies of Drach (1969) and other students of Slobin. The published output goes back only to 1972, with the reports of Moerk (1972) and Snow (1972). Finality in the categorization of instructional forms and exhaustiveness in their recognition has certainly not yet been achieved. The results to be presented will therefore probably be underestimates of the actual intensity of instruction. As discussed in the method section, it was attempted in the present taxonomy to incorporate the best analyses from the field and to add to them and improve upon them wherever it seemed required.

The arrangement of the maternal instructional techniques will be somewhat different in the subsequent tables than it was presented in Table 5. This was done to better assemble the variety of procedures into a few linguistically meaningful sets. The subdivision in the following table is, however, not yet fully satisfactory. It will be seen that the criterion for inclusion of categories in Table 16 is the imitative character of the maternal utterance, i.e., an interactional feature. For Tables 17, 18, and 19, the criteria for inclusion are linguistic, i.e., the type of linguistic skill taught; in Table 20 the criterion is again mainly interactional; and finally, Table 21 contains two waste-basket categories. Decades of work will probably be needed to arrive at an esthetically beautiful and logically simple system of instructional techniques. But if the work is not begun despite imperfections, the goal never will be reached.

Table 16 focuses upon maternal imitation techniques. They are relatively finely differentiated. Almost all types of linguistic skills could be taught by means of imitation, since the maternal imitation is rarely an exact one but is mostly phonetically, morphologically, and syntactically improved. Even the imitation coded as 1 and labelled "identical" is not really identical but very often phonetically improved. Many of the phonetic improvements were certainly lost, since the transcriptions were made on a normal typewriter and could not capture fine phonetic differences. The overall frequency of imitation, $N = 1640$, and the frequencies per hour, certainly are impressive and probably important for Eve's language acquisition, as has been suggested by

TABLE 16

Maternal Techniques Mainly Involving Repetition of Parts or All of the Child's Preceding Utterance(s)

Instruction technique	Code	Sa[a] 1	Sa 3	Sa 5	Sa 7	Sa 9	Sa 11	Sa 13	Sa 15	Sa 17	Sa 19	Total of 20 hrs	r[b] w/age	r w/MLU	Multiple R
Identical & reduced imitation	01	18	11	33	31	19	17	27	70	35	43	304	.13	.13	.13
Expanding imitation	02	41	32	92	103	71	40	54	76	51	63	623	-.65	-.69	.71
Structural imitation	03	0	0	0	0	0	0	0	0	1	0	1	c		
Imitation with substitution of items	04	1	8	10	21	10	3	18	26	27	21	145	.56	.58	.59
Combinatory imitation	05	1	2	1	2	1	3	4	13	1	5	33	.35	.44	.61
Incorporating imitation	06	60	30	32	40	14	6	14	18	14	6	234	-.79	-.80	.80
Chaining or coupling	07	2	8	3	8	2	9	25	44	33	38	172	.86	.86	.86
Two-person sentence	08	0	0	1	1	2	1	4	5	2	1	17	.51	.50	.51
Imitation & self-rep.	09	9	10	16	14	3	4	9	16	11	8	100	-.80	-.77	.80
Quotation	10	0	0	3	1	0	0	0	4	4	1	13	c		
Total imit. tech.		132	101	191	221	122	83	155	272	179	186	1640	-.80	-.81	.81

[a]Two hours per sample were analyzed.
[b]All correlations were computed from the percentages of frequencies in order to equalize for varying sample lengths.
[c]There were too many cells with zero frequencies to compute meaningful correlation coefficients.

several of the specific analyses in preceding tables and by a few studies on imitation in the literature (Bloom et al., 1974; Clark, 1977; Moerk, 1977; Moerk et al., 1979). Considering specific types of imitation and their developmental trends, it has to be kept in mind that the type of imitation is to a considerable extent a function of the child's utterance that is to be imitated. The decline in Incorporating Imitation is, for example, probably due to the decrease in one word utterances of the child. If the child does not produce many of these one-word utterances, the mother cannot produce many Incorporating Imitations, since these presuppose definitionally one-word utterances. Similarly, the relative decline in Expanding Imitation, code 2, is to a large degree a function of the omission of functors in the utterances of the child. The more the child supplies these functors, the fewer Expanding Imitations the mother will produce—almost by definition. The third declining trend in Imitation plus Self-repetition, code 9, is probably an indirect function of the child's increasing linguistic skills, since this form represents almost a maximum of redundancy. If such redundancy is less needed, a decline in maternal production of this form could be expected. Considering the increasing trends for Imitation with Substitution of Items (4), Combinatory Imitation (5), Chaining or Coupling (7), and marginally for Two-person Sentences (8), it is apparent that these are more complex forms of imitation. Items from two or more utterances of one or both partners are combined, or item substitutions are made in producing the new utterance. Finally, categories 3 and 10, Structural Imitation and Quotation, were conceived mainly for the coding of Eve's utterances and they are consequently quite rare in the maternal speech. As is to be expected when imitation is considered as a provision of redundancy, total imitations decline with the development of the child.

With the exception of Morpheme Perseveration, code 24, which deals with bound morphemes and therefore word-constituent structure, all techniques summarized in Table 17 serve predominantly to clarify the constituent structure of single clauses. This can be accomplished through simple repetition, code 20, which gives the child another opportunity to analyze the sentence structure. More often it is done by means of sophisticated manipulation of constituents of the sentence, that is, addition, deletion, or replacement. An instructionally important phenomenon is encountered in what was labeled "Structural Mapping," code 51, that is, the almost exact mapping of a situational structure which is clearly observed and comprehended by the child into a linguistic structure. Finally, some form of mapping is involved when, in a similar manner, two linguistic structures are equivalent in expressing the same message but differ in syntax, which was coded as 52, Meaning Parallels and Structural Contrasts. Both the frequency of all clause-teaching techniques per hour, i.e., over 200, and also the frequencies of each technique over the 20 hours of analysis, are considerable. It is evident from the transcripts and from Brown's analyses that Eve was progressing quite rap-

TABLE 17

Maternal Techniques Spontaneously Modeling and Elaborating Simple Clause Structures

Instruction technique	Code	Sa[a] 1	Sa 3	Sa 5	Sa 7	Sa 9	Sa 11	Sa 13	Sa 15	Sa 17	Sa 19	Total of 20 hrs	r^b w/age	r w/MLU	Multiple R
Repeats own statement	20	17	18	20	18	13	10	21	24	27	6	174	−.80	−.81	.81
Completions	21	1	0	5	6	4	2	5	13	7	7	50	.68	.68	.68
Build-up sequence	22	23	24	35	43	24	15	31	39	44	14	292	−.84	−.85	.85
Break-down sequence	23	19	26	43	51	12	13	42	57	48	28	339	−.50	−.47	.50
Morpheme perseveration	24[c]	0	53	16	42	56	42	114	267	151	181	922	.86	.90	.92
Replacement: constituents	25	45	69	97	125	55	22	95	77	102	78	765	−.64	−.64	.64
Replacement: minor elem.	26	0	10	6	35	4	13	30	27	40	22	187	.48	.46	.48
Frame variation	27	39	56	66	100	40	59	99	128	91	103	781	−.11	−.13	.16
Structural mapping	51	24	33	63	50	31	22	59	97	49	25	453	−.67	−.62	.69
Meaning parallels; structural contrasts	52	0	13	12	11	5	6	18	9	16	4	94	−.14	−.14	.14
Total clause teaching techniques		168	302	363	481	244	204	514	738	575	468	4057	−.02	.01	.15

[a]Two hours per sample were analyzed.
[b]All correlations were computed from the percentages of frequencies in order to equalize for varying sample lengths.
[c]Morpheme perseveration was coded in this category independently of whether it was spontaneous or in imitation of the child's production.

idly during the period under consideration in her mastery of the simple sentence structure. It is therefore developmentally meaningful that all the techniques which are mainly concerned with sentence constituents decline in relative frequency in the mother's input. In contrast to this, the Replacement of Minor Constituents, code 26, and Morpheme Perseveration, code 24, increase in relative frequency, and it is well known from Brown's analysis that Eve gradually acquired various bound and minor free morphemes during this period.

From a certain point on in her development, the child has also to learn to deal with more complex sentences and relations between sentences. Obviously input is necessary for this. It would be quite impossible to deal in a small report like the present one with the entire topic of the acquisition of complex sentences. Only a few of the most interesting aspects of the probably relevant input can therefore be summarized in Table 18.

Table 18 contains data on only two major types of complexity: optional transformations within one clause and subordination of clauses. These two instructional forms increase in relative and absolute frequencies with the linguistic development of Eve. In the case of the somewhat simpler optional transformations, mainly question and negation transformations, the input is already relatively intense at the beginning of the recording period. For the more complex type of subordination, the mother begins at zero in sample 1. It is fascinating to note how she provides increasingly frequent models of subordination for around 13 samples before she invites the child to perform this feat herself in asking her several questions that require an adverbial clause as answer. The latter is seen from sample 15 on. It will be remembered from Table 17 that most of the simple clause teaching methods declined with Eve's development. For the more complex syntactic forms, Table 18 shows that the teaching increases relatively and even more absolutely with Eve's development. Both trends fit in well with Eve's level of syntactic development. Since, in Table 18, the correlation patterns for code 28 and for the Total suggested net suppression, the partial correlations were computed. They are positive with age, $r = .49$ and $.44$, respectively, and negative with MLU $-.43$ and $-.30$, respectively. This correlation pattern is certainly interesting insofar as the mother's underlying rationale might be concerned. Since it was not expected, it is deemed preferable to shy away from post-hoc speculations.

Beginning developmentally earlier but continuing throughout all of life is the next task to be considered, i.e., the acquisition and enlargement of the vocabulary repertoire. Especially in this case, there is no question that input and rote learning must be of greatest importance. Table 19 summarizes some input phenomena encountered in the maternal management of this task.

In accordance with the above mentioned expectation, Table 19 shows that rehearsal, code 29, is most frequent numerically. With over 800 instances in 20 hours of interaction on the mother's side alone—a later study

TABLE 18

Maternal Techniques Demonstrating Optional Transformations

Instruction technique	Code	Sa[a] 1	Sa 3	Sa 5	Sa 7	Sa 9	Sa 11	Sa 13	Sa 15	Sa 17	Sa 19	Total of 20 hrs	r[b] w/age	r w/MLU	Multiple R
Optional transformation	28	27	39	43	71	47	43	70	72	97	103	612	.34	.25	.60
Elaboration with adverbial clause	58	0	5	2	14	4	9	19	23	30	27	133	.85	.81	.86
Asks a question requiring an adverbial clause	59	0	2	0	0	0	0	1	18	7	5	33	[c]		
Total techniques for teaching complex syntax		27	46	45	85	51	52	90	113	134	135	778	.64	.58	.71

[a]Two hours per sample were analyzed.
[b]All correlations were computed from the percentages of frequencies in order to equalize for varying sample lengths.
[c]There were too many cells with zero frequencies to compute meaningful correlation coefficients.

49

TABLE 19
Maternal Techniques Serving Mainly Vocabulary Instruction

Instruction technique	Code	Sa[a] 1	Sa 3	Sa 5	Sa 7	Sa 9	Sa 11	Sa 13	Sa 15	Sa 17	Sa 19	Total of 20 hrs	r[b] w/age	r w/MLU	Multiple R
Perseveration of vocabulary	29	37	60	76	48	59	14	73	255	107	103	832	.14	.26	.68
Provides labels	50	17	6	23	7	2	1	19	20	20	8	123	-.45	-.49	.52
Asks for labels	53	15	5	34	8	4	4	7	10	6	2	95	-.71	-.74	.75
Asks "What doing" question	54	7	5	7	10	13	5	8	21	8	5	89	-.48	-.45	.49
Feature elaboration	55	4	2	6	5	2	8	18	21	18	4	88	.35	.29	.45
Dynamic elaboration	56	1	2	9	3	1	3	2	12	7	3	43	.05	.06	.09
Functional elaboration	57	4	8	6	3	1	1	3	8	6	0	40	-.68	-.62	.72
Encoding of internal states	71	0	0	4	0	6	0	7	0	24	15	56	.65	.58	.80
Total vocabulary teaching techniques		85	88	165	84	88	36	137	347	196	140	1366	-.19	-.14	.32

[a]Two hours per sample were analyzed.
[b]All correlations were computed from the percentages of frequencies in order to equalize for varying sample lengths.

will show that the child is almost equally active in rehearsing, $N = 714$—Eve encounters on the average two repetitions of rare vocabulary items every 3 minutes in the input alone. The reader is reminded that only those vocabulary items were counted that appeared to the coders new and rare from their knowledge of the transcripts. Rehearsal and reinstatement of relatively familiar items could and will often have been overlooked, so that the total frequencies must be much higher. Whereas all the other categories in Table 19 are much less frequent, their frequency rank order and their developmental trends are of considerable interest and also of psychological significance. Codes 50 and 53 dealing with simple labels are most common, then follow those codes capturing verb teaching: codes 54, 56, and 57. Last follow code 55, Feature Elaboration, dealing mainly with adjective teaching, and code 71, the encoding of internal states. In regard to this last code, a possible source of error has, however, to be mentioned. The need for this code was only discovered when the computer coding of the samples was already far progressed. This category was therefore incorporated in the coding manual only during the coding of the later samples. Although all the samples were rechecked for the incidence of pertinent items, it is possible that during the process of the more speedy rechecking some instances of code 71 were overlooked. Neither the frequencies for individual samples nor the developmental trend should therefore be relied upon too heavily. Since under category 71 were coded mostly the verbs *think, believe, know,* etc., the trend makes psychological sense; but it needs reevaluation with other dyads and with a fixed method for coding.

The other developmental trends also appear quite meaningful from a developmental point of view: The training of nouns declines quite steeply. Both the simple *What are you doing* question and the Functional Elaboration decline too. This appears adjusted to Eve's linguistic growth, since both techniques deal with simple activities of the child or those that can be performed with objects in her environment. Eve will more and more master these verbs. Technique 56, Dynamic Elaboration, seems to have been used predominantly by Eve's mother in connection with objects, including animate objects, seen in books, where they could be involved in more exotic activities. The learning of new verbs is therefore more probable in this context. This last impression needs, however, systematic evaluation, since it derives only from the intuitive knowledge of the transcripts. Finally, Table 19 might also explain why adjectives are acquired comparatively late by many children. Feature Elaboration, code 55, that pertains mainly to adjective teaching, is encountered in the average only around 4 times per hour of interaction.

The trend for code 29, Perseveration of Vocabulary Items, appears quite flat upon first impression. This would make sense, since it is a composite of all the other trends in Table 19. The high multiple R indicates, however, that a case of net suppression is encountered here too and that the partial correlations need to be considered. They are − .59 and .62 with age and MLU, respectively. Since a considerable variety of linguistic and psychological factors are entailed in vocabulary perseveration, an unambiguous explanation of this correlation pattern cannot be offered. But it fits well with established psychological knowledge: Memory improvement with age would lead to a decreasing need for rehearsal, but increased language skills would result in the introduction of more vocabulary items and therefore also in more frequent 29 codes. Though for codes 55 and 71 signs of net suppression are encountered too, these trends seem too unclear or uncertain to deserve detailed exploration.

Whereas in the preceding tables the spontaneous provision of linguistic information by the mother was considered, Table 20 is oriented towards the question of how the mother responds to Eve's language production so as to inform her of the adequacy of her linguistic productions.

Of greatest theoretical interest, since it was often a topic of controversy, and of greatest importance in regard to frequency is code 80, Feedback as to Correctness, which would in learning-theoretical terms be labelled conditioned positive reinforcement. In the average, Eve's mother responds once every 2 minutes with a positive remark about her child's linguistic productions. Since the child is still very much in the period of language learning, though she progresses to more complex tasks, it makes psychologically eminent sense that the developmental trend is almost completely flat. Since the correlation pattern suggests classical suppression, the partial correlations are of interest. They are − .25 for age and .25 for MLU, which again makes sense psychologically: If the child did not progress to more complex linguistic constructions, the mother would decrease her positive reinforcement with increasing age of the child. If code 80 can be considered as conditioned positive reinforcement, code 81 reflects conditioned punishment. The mother begins almost at the zero level when Eve is still in her early stages of language mastery—so as not to discourage her, it could be speculated—and clearly increases her negative responses to the child's linguistic productions. The positive responses are, however, on the average four times as frequent.

Since Eve succeeds gradually in formulating her verbal messages more clearly, the mother's Feedback as to Clarity, code 60, can steeply decrease with Eve's development. Contrasting correction, code 40, follows a trend very similar to that of the more obvious correction, code 81. Being less damaging for the child's motivation, since it is less obvious, contrasting correction is provided by the mother more often, around ten instances per hour. In addition, as will be seen in a subsequent section, the mother employs a clever camouflage technique to lessen the bite of the correction provided: She precedes or follows the utterance coded 40 by conditioned positive reinforcement, code 80. Thereby she tells Eve: "Yes, I like your utterance; it is good, but a minor improvement is needed in . . . ." Challenge, code 41, is

TABLE 20

Maternal Techniques Providing Positive, Critical, or Negative Feedback

Instruction technique	Code	Sa[a] 1	Sa 3	Sa 5	Sa 7	Sa 9	Sa 11	Sa 13	Sa 15	Sa 17	Sa 19	Total of 20 hrs	r^b w/age	r w/MLU	Multiple R
Contrasting correction	40	2	2	21	24	18	14	40	39	32	17	209	.49	.43	.57
Challenge	41	3	1	0	9	0	0	4	10	2	7	36	.03	.09	.37
Feedback as to clarity	60	18	7	14	23	19	3	11	12	10	11	128	−.68	−.70	.70
Item specification	61	7	11	45	26	11	26	30	81	40	52	329	.51	.50	.51
Feedback as to correctness	80	27	39	68	52	42	23	47	91	41	44	474	−.05	.01	.31
Feedback as to mistakes	81	2	0	7	11	14	5	25	28	15	15	122	.64	.62	.64
Total Feedback		59	60	155	145	104	71	157	261	140	146	1298	−.08	−.09	.14

[a]Two hours per sample were analyzed.
[b]All correlations were computed from the percentages of frequencies in order to equalize for varying sample lengths.

53

too infrequent to be of importance. Why Item Specification, code 61, should developmentally increase needs to be investigated by recourse to the actual utterances. The correlation pattern for code 40 indicates net suppression and deserves therefore to be explored. The partial correlation with age is positive, $r = .38$. and that with MLU is negative, $r = -.29$. Adapted where needed, the argument proferred for code 80 pertains equally to this net suppression in code 40.

Finally, and for completeness' sake, two waste-basket categories have to be briefly considered. They are summarized in Table 21 as Other and Uncodable. As the definition of Other, code 99, in Table 5 suggests, considerable phonetic/phonological and other teaching techniques could be subsumed under this heading. Since a variety of phenomena is included, little can be said about the steeply declining developmental trend besides the fact that most utterances fell increasingly under the well-defined categories. Since Uncodable was employed mainly to code gaps in the transcript that signified that an utterance was incomprehensible from the tape, the slightly declining trend might indicate a clearer conversational structure which allowed the transcriber better to interpret the maternal utterances on the tape. Since the partial correlation with MLU is positive, however, $r = .28$, it might be best to avoid attempts at interpretation.

Frequencies of sequential pairs of utterances. Whereas it is certainly hoped that the preceding evidence about maternal instructional techniques might provide some valuable insights into the processes of language instruction, the following sections are considered more important for the understanding of the processes transpiring in mother-child dyads. In these sections the emphasis will be upon contingencies of maternal and filial verbal behaviors. First, simple pairs will be considered, and toward the end the first suggestions as to longer sequences will be presented. Before the relatively unexplored topic concerning the contingencies between maternal instructional techniques and the child's learning strategies is investigated, a brief presentation of the contingencies of the illocutionary force categories will be provided. This presentation of very familiar patterns with a little used methodology will not only provide a good grasp of the character of the interactions between Eve and her mother but will also lay the foundation for the later interpretations of instructional and learning processes on the basis of the employed methodology.

In Table 22 are presented the 10 most frequent pairs of utterances that follow the pattern: child begins - mother responds. The patterns found are obviously in good correspondence with intuitive expectations: Declarative - Affirmation; Declarative - Agreement; Declarative - Clarifying Query, etc. For a grasp of the emotional climate in the interactions, the sum of Affirmations and Agreements, i.e., the sum of maternal agreements, $N = 400$, can be com-

TABLE 21

Categories for Uncodable Items in the Mother's Speech

Instruction technique	Code	Sa[a] 1	Sa 3	Sa 5	Sa 7	Sa 9	Sa 11	Sa 13	Sa 15	Sa 17	Sa 19	Total of 20 hrs	r[b] w/age	r w/MLU	Multiple R
Other	99	32	34	53	63	32	28	52	68	35	48	445	-.87	-.87	.87
Uncodable	00	21	47	41	63	29	18	53	74	66	67	479	-.22	-.16	.36

[a]Two hours per sample were analyzed.
[b]All correlations were computed from the percentages of frequencies in order to equalize for varying sample lengths.

TABLE 22

The Most Common Pairs of Illocutionary Force Items with
the Child's Utterance as Antecedent

Pattern	Sa[a] 1	Sa 3	Sa 5	Sa 7	Sa 9	Sa 11	Sa 13	Sa 15	Sa 17	Sa 19	Total of 20 hrs	r[b] w/age	r w/MLU	Multiple R
Declarative - affirmation	13	18	16	21	30	13	17	38	23	22	211	-.25	-.22	.28
Declarative - agreement	6	7	29	18	10	10	12	58	21	18	189	.27	.35	.53
Declarative - clarifying	5	3	12	10	16	7	19	37	13	15	137	.48	.50	.50
Question - answer	4	3	17	8	7	5	30	26	19	16	135	.53	.47	.59
Request - compliance	4	5	10	13	7	4	3	28	5	7	86	-.16	-.01	.82
Answer - clarifying	4	3	8	9	5	8	5	20	8	8	78	.16	.18	.20
Declarative - declarative	3	7	14	5	6	7	8	12	7	7	76	-.28	-.30	.32
Request - clarifying	8	6	7	17	7	2	6	14	0	3	70	-.76	-.68	.84
Request - refusal	3	7	11	18	12	0	9	8	0	2	70	-.55	-.50	.60
Declarative - disagreement	4	2	4	6	6	7	5	15	9	8	66	.34	.31	.36

[a]Two hours per sample were analyzed.
[b]All correlations were computed from the percentages of frequencies in order to equalize for varying sample lengths.

56

pared with the small number of maternal disagreements, i.e., Declarative - Disagreement, namely 66. Declarative - Negation with a total of 35 instances in 20 hours doesn't even appear under the first 10 patterns. It is of interest how often the mother still needs to respond with a clarifying query to the statements of the child, $N = 285$. The developmental trends of these patterns with Clarifying Query in the second slot, labeled 'Clarifying' in the tables, need more intensive investigation since they go in different directions. An increasing trend in response to declarative statements, i.e., Declarative - Clarifying contrasts with a steeply decreasing trend in response to Eve's requests, Request - Clarifying, and a relatively flat pattern in response to Eve's answers, Answer - Clarifying. The predominance of maternal positive responses over negative ones is again seen in the patterns of compliance versus refusal in response to a request of Eve, i.e., Request - Compliance versus Request - Refusal. The relationship is 86 to 70; but these numbers do not tell the entire story because all the Request - Clarifying pairs as well as some other chains involving clarification sequences end in compliance or refusal. The total predominance of compliance over refusal is therefore probably higher.

It is instructive to contrast and compare the patterns just described with those observed when the first utterance of the pair is produced by the mother. The 10 most frequent pairs are presented in Table 23.

There are only two identical code patterns in both tables, namely Question - Answer and Declarative - Declarative. The latter is much rarer when the mother responds, since, as the later analyses of triplets will show, the mother takes care to acknowlege the child's declarative utterance before she adds her own. When contrasting the two tables, the mother's greater versatility is obvious. Whereas Eve asked mainly simple questions to obtain new information, when she asked any, the mother employs testing questions, and the clarifying query besides the simple question form. Whereas Eve introduced 8 of the 10 most frequent pairs with only two types of utterances, i.e., Declarative and Request, and she employed altogether in those 10 most frequent pairs only four types of utterances, her mother employed seven different illocutionary types and only two of them appear in two pairs each.

Considering Table 23 by itself, the frequency of testing questions followed by an answer of Eve is impressive. It is evident that Eve has already learned the conversational pattern of question-answer, i.e., Testing - Answer, Question - Answer, Clarifying - Answer. The sum of these pairs is 338. Quite a few of the mother's clarifying queries are answered by an Affirmation or with a full Answer. The pattern Affirmation - Declarative and the less frequent Agreement - Declarative demonstrate that the mother's positive acceptance of the child's preceding utterance leads to further declarative statements by Eve. The pattern Question - Affirmation that might seem astonishing at first, is seen as highly meaningful when the transcripts are studied. It arises from the fact that the mother often guesses correctly the child's ideas

TABLE 23

The Most Common Pairs of Illocutionary Force Items with the Mother's Utterance as Antecedent

Pattern	Sa[a] 1	Sa 3	Sa 5	Sa 7	Sa 9	Sa 11	Sa 13	Sa 15	Sa 17	Sa 19	Total of 20 hrs	r^b w/age	r w/MLU	Multiple R
Declarative - declarative	8	5	19	11	19	20	28	34	25	28	197	.51	.42	.69
Testing - answer	7	4	39	22	0	12	8	38	17	14	161	-.06	-.06	.06
Affirmation - declarative	0	4	10	11	12	7	9	33	13	15	114	.66	.72	.76
Question - answer	3	6	5	7	10	7	14	28	12	17	109	.73	.77	.78
Clarifying- declarative	7	9	11	9	13	3	9	25	11	11	108	-.25	-.17	.48
Prescribing - declarative	7	10	14	8	3	1	8	15	10	14	90	-.36	-.32	.42
Question - affirmation	1	6	14	11	4	2	14	13	6	12	83	.18	.20	.23
Clarifying - affirmation	0	4	8	8	5	3	3	19	9	14	73	.64	.71	.79
Declarative - repetitive	8	8	17	7	8	1	13	2	4	1	69	-.77	-.81	.81
Clarifying - answer	4	1	4	6	8	11	10	12	5	7	68	.23	.17	.37

[a]Two hours per sample were analyzed.
[b]All correlations were computed from the percentages of frequencies in order to equalize for varying sample lengths.

and wishes: e.g., Mother: *Do you want peanut butter on your bread?* Eve: *Yes*. Since two independent variables, the two codes, are involved in each case, it is quite risky to speculate about the implications of the developmental trends. Only the steeply declining trend in the pattern Declarative - Repetitive, a maternal declarative utterance being followed by Eve's imitation without illocutionary force, is quite clearly due to the decline in Eve's non-functional imitations. The many increasing trends reflect probably a routinization of the conversational interaction, i.e., that Eve acquires more and more the conversational rules of how to respond to maternal utterance categories. This is suggested since the trends demonstrate increases in relative frequencies, that is, less dispersion in the responses of Eve to specific maternal utterances. These trends might, of course, change at later periods, when the child develops more versatility in her illocutionary repertoire.

Finally, it happens quite often that the mother sees fit to produce two or more utterances between those of Eve. These patterns resulting from pairs of maternal utterances are presented in Table 24.

Double declaratives might represent some redundancy or reflect the need for simple sentences, since they decline somewhat with development. The high frequency of the pairs Affirmation - Agreement and Agreement - Affirmation is almost an artifact of the coding system, since the "yes" before or after an agreeing utterance was coded separately. It pertains, however, certainly to the discussion found in various sections of the study concerning the importance of positive conditioned reinforcement. These frequencies should be compared with the frequency of Negation - Disagreement, that is, doubly expressed disagreement, which is much less common, the proportions being 250:60. In a similar manner, double compliance is more common than double refusal. That parents often need to repeat their commands, Prescribing - Prescribing, is common enough knowledge, though this need declines with Eve's age, the partial correlation with age being −.43. Interestingly, the double compliances and the double refusals decline with age too, the partial correlations being −.46 and −.57. The partial correlations with MLU for the last three pairs are .39, .36, and .45, respectively. This seems to indicate again, as suggested in a previous section, the tendency in this household of graduate students to handle upcoming interactional concerns verbally as soon as the child is linguistically ready for it. For the entire Table 24, the correlation patterns are quite complicated, and with only two exceptions, that is Agreement - Affirmation and Affirmation - Agreement classical or net suppression is encountered. Without further studies, speculations about the psychological meaning of the trends indicated by the partial correlations would be risky. The partial correlations are therefore not presented. But keeping in mind that the correlation between age and MLU is .98, all the information needed is found in the tables to compute the partial correlations (cf. Cohen & Cohen, 1975, pp. 78ff), if any reader should need them to evaluate special hypotheses.

TABLE 24

The Most Common Pairs of Illocutionary Force Items Produced
by the Mother in Immediate Succession

Pattern	Sa[a] 1	Sa 3	Sa 5	Sa 7	Sa 9	Sa 11	Sa 13	Sa 15	Sa 17	Sa 19	Total of 20 hrs	r^b w/age	r w/MLU	Multiple R
Declarative - declarative	11	19	26	32	14	9	14	27	37	15	204	-.12	-.15	.24
Affirmation - agreement	19	18	17	9	16	6	11	17	16	16	145	-.69	-.70	.70
Agreement - affirmation	6	6	22	18	5	6	4	19	10	9	105	-.47	-.45	.48
Prescribing - prescribing	5	10	10	9	7	1	12	19	12	7	92	-.28	-.20	.49
Compliance - compliance	7	13	6	13	4	7	4	14	7	8	83	-.58	-.51	.67
Declarative - prescribing	3	14	6	12	2	6	11	9	7	10	80	-.32	-.28	.39
Disagreement - declarative	4	1	4	2	7	6	14	14	16	7	75	.53	.43	.73
Prescribing - declarative	0	9	5	14	2	1	10	8	11	6	66	.01	.06	.29
Negation - disagreement	4	0	4	5	5	6	6	11	11	8	60	.39	.29	.66
Refusal - refusal	7	6	4	20	5	0	5	10	0	1	58	-.67	-.59	.78

[a]Two hours per sample were analyzed.
[b]All correlations were computed from the percentages of frequencies in order to equalize for varying sample lengths.

After a flavor of the illocutionary patterns in the interactions of Eve and her mother has been conveyed, the attention will again be centered upon the main topic, the maternal teaching techniques and the child's learning strategies. In Table 25, the child's strategy introduces the pair and it is followed by a maternal technique.

Eve's vocabulary perseveration, code 29, and the maternal responses to it, are most frequent and shall be considered first. Vocabulary acquisition is naturally in no way completed at the upper limit of the period studied, and the patterns are still increasing in absolute frequency. A clear relative decline is, however, seen in those patterns, wherein the mother only rewards or repeats the vocabulary item in the same syntactic structure, i.e., 29–80 and 29–2. In contrast, repetition of the rare word, 29–29, often in new sentence frames, is slightly increasing as a percentage, and a pattern that demands considerable information processing on the side of the child, i.e., 29–24, vocabulary perseveration followed by bound morpheme perseveration, is increasing steeply with Eve's development. Parallel to the trends in vocabulary-training/learning go those that pertain to attempts to code situational structures with syntactic structures, i.e., code 51 followed by a maternal technique. The patterns involving simple maternal responses, i.e., 51–80 and 51–2, decline with Eve's development. In contrast, 51–51 and 51–24 exhibit increasing trends. Since the correlational patterns of the last two pairs indicate suppression, the relationships are more complex. For 51–51, the partial correlation with age is $-.67$, and with MLU it is $.70$. For the pair 51–24, the respective correlations are $-.59$ and $.72$. Both pairs show therefore an increasing trend with MLU and a declining one with age, if MLU is partialled out. Again no attempt will be made to offer post-hoc speculations to explain these trends, since no specific trends had been hypothesized.

Contemplating these most frequent doubles in Table 25 together, the leftmost column reads almost as if it had been composed by a grammarian and were not the result of casual mother-child conversations. The child's codes will be first considered: 29 deals with vocabulary acquisition; 51, 21, 25, and 22 concern mainly the larger syntactic units; and 24 is specifically a code indicating the learning of bound morphemes. The mother employs two major principles in responding to Eve's learning endeavors: She makes certain to often add a reward, code 80, and she relies much upon repetition; i.e., codes 29, 2, and 24. In repeating a preceding utterance, she has three options: she can concentrate mainly upon the vocabulary item, code 29; mainly upon the bound morphemes, code 24; or she can repeat an entire sentence, code 2, and add minor free and bound morphemes.

Table 26 contains those patterns that were introduced by an utterance of the mother followed by one of Eve. It is most impressive if first of all the close similarity between column one in Table 26 and the same column in Table 25 is considered. The only new code is that of 27, frame variation, that is being in-

TABLE 25
The Most Common Pairs of Strategy/Technique Items
with the Child's Utterance as Antecedent

Pattern	Sa[a] 1	Sa 3	Sa 5	Sa 7	Sa 9	Sa 11	Sa 13	Sa 15	Sa 17	Sa 19	Total of 20 hrs	r[b] w/age	r w/MLU	Multiple R
29–29	6	15	9	5	12	3	18	75	26	28	197	.18	.19	.19
29–80	4	10	12	3	10	2	11	26	13	10	101	-.36	-.38	.38
51–2	2	4	14	20	13	9	3	20	10	5	100	-.26	-.29	.32
24–24	0	1	0	0	2	3	9	45	11	27	98	.84	.83	.84
29–24	0	3	1	0	3	1	10	42	7	20	87	.73	.74	.74
51–80	1	7	8	9	13	6	7	22	5	8	86	-.25	-.26	.26
2–80	4	11	18	12	10	3	9	7	5	5	84	-.78	-.77	.78
25–2	4	4	14	11	13	6	2	8	7	10	79	-.53	-.59	.65
29–2	4	8	6	3	8	3	0	20	6	17	75	-.47	-.45	.47
22–2	4	5	8	14	6	5	11	5	4	3	65	-.70	-.72	.72
51–51	0	2	8	11	1	5	3	27	6	2	65	.28	.41	.79
51–24	0	3	1	0	1	3	3	24	13	11	59	.69	.78	.89

[a]Two hours per sample were analyzed.
[b]All correlations were computed from the percentages of frequencies in order to equalize for varying sample lengths.

TABLE 26

The Most Common Pairs[c] of Strategy/Technique Items with the Mother's Utterance as Antecedent

Pattern	Sa[a] 1	Sa 3	Sa 5	Sa 7	Sa 9	Sa 11	Sa 13	Sa 15	Sa 17	Sa 19	Total of 20 hrs	r[b] w/age	r w/MLU	Multiple R
29–29	8	8	18	6	12	3	18	48	14	25	160	.02	.07	.30
24–29	0	9	1	0	10	4	6	39	12	17	98	.43	.53	.74
24–24	0	0	0	1	6	2	9	33	10	28	89	.85	.88	.89
25–2	3	7	22	11	8	2	8	4	8	7	80	-.54	-.55	.55
27–2	4	8	11	11	6	3	9	11	6	7	76	-.79	-.75	.81
27–29	2	9	3	4	4	4	8	17	12	11	74	.00	.07	.37
24–51	0	1	4	4	6	4	4	32	7	7	69	.54	.63	.76
25–29	3	10	6	4	11	0	1	16	5	10	66	-.37	-.29	.57
29–2	4	6	15	7	3	0	5	9	4	8	61	-.63	-.60	.63
51–2	5	2	22	3	3	3	6	8	4	2	58	-.52	-.57	.60

[a]Two hours per sample were analyzed.

[b]All correlations were computed from the percentages of frequencies in order to equalize for varying sample lengths.

[c]This description is not completely adequate, since the pairs 27–0, 24–0, 29–0, 25–0, and 28–0 ranked 2, 4, 5, 8, and 13, respectively. Since these pairs suggest only that the child might not have been able to cope with the maternal input, they were omitted.

troduced by the mother. Table 26 shows again the grammarian's ideal of training in vocabulary, morphology, and the analysis, code 25, and synthesis, code 51, of sentences. The mother is adding, however, a note of complexity as indicated by the code 27. It will be remembered that 27, frame variation, encompasses a variety of syntactic transformations which can be simple word order change with retained meaning, word order change with changed meaning, or often even a change in sentence frames, from full-verb to copula sentence or vice versa with retained meaning. Considerable syntactic learning must be possible as a consequence of these maternal models. Since this argument seems to be in contrast with the flat developmental curve for 27–29 and the steep decline for 27–2, the correlation patterns need to be closely examined. The correlation pattern for the pair 27–29 indicates classical suppression. The partial correlations are $-.34$ with age and $.35$ with MLU, indicating that the increase in the frequency of the pair with Eve's language level is suppressed by the decrease due to the age factor. The decline with age is probably due to the strategy of the child encountered in the pair. Vocabulary perseveration, code 29, is one of the simplest strategies Eve employed when her capacities were overtaxed by the maternal input; i.e., she simply repeated one word that was rare or new. With only very minor changes, this argument should also apply to the pair 27–2. Code 2, like code 29, represents abbreviated imitation differing only in degree of abbreviation. The partial correlations are very comparable, $-.42$ with age and $.46$ with MLU. If the above arguments are correct, then the MLU-related increase would be due to the technique 27 employed by the mother. But, as with all these interpretations, the above ones are really more speculations, or at best hypotheses to be evaluated in the future.

Trying to abstract some general principles from most of the trends, relationships similar to those in Table 25 appear: Patterns containing only simple techniques/strategies have a tendency to decline with development, whereas patterns with more demanding strategies/techniques either increase obviously as in those containing 24, or demonstrate a complex and differential relationship with the two independent variables.

Finally, instances were often encountered when one verbal intervention of the mother was followed by a second one of hers, resulting in two techniques in sequence. The most frequent pairs of two successive maternal techniques are presented in Table 27.

Considered from a dynamic perspective, Table 27 suggests what the most difficult areas for language acquisition might be, wherein the mother has to try especially hard to help Eve to master them. Table 27 presents quite a different picture from that of Tables 25 and 26. Of course, there is still the unending task of vocabulary instruction and learning, code 29–29, but the emphasis is clearly upon more complex topics: Five of the eleven pairs serve the task of instruction in functors, i.e., they contain codes 24 or 2; five of the

TABLE 27

The Most Common Pairs of Technique Items Produced by the Mother in Immediate Succession

Pattern	Sa[a] 1	Sa 3	Sa 5	Sa 7	Sa 9	Sa 11	Sa 13	Sa 15	Sa 17	Sa 19	Total of 20 hrs	r[b] w/age	r w/MLU	Multiple R
24–24	0	3	0	5	8	9	17	42	33	28	145	.94	.93	.94
29–29	7	8	11	11	7	3	12	43	15	13	130	-.25	-.13	.69
25–25	4	13	9	39	4	1	16	4	17	7	114	-.35	-.31	.39
27–27	3	9	4	16	4	9	16	16	9	16	102	-.09	-.04	.25
28–28	5	7	2	11	14	5	14	8	17	13	96	-.14	-.19	.33
28–25	3	9	7	10	7	2	16	3	18	11	86	-.18	-.20	.22
24–25	0	7	1	6	3	1	10	17	17	19	81	.65	.69	.71
24–27	0	6	0	3	6	6	13	22	11	14	81	.64	.67	.69
29–27	6	5	5	4	4	4	9	25	10	7	79	-.30	-.26	.36
28–24	0	3	1	5	6	6	8	9	18	14	70	.69	.62	.77
2–25	8	3	9	14	9	3	7	3	8	5	69	-.72	-.76	.78

[a]Two hours per sample were analyzed.
[b]All correlations were computed from the percentages of frequencies in order to equalize for varying sample lengths.

eleven pairs contain explicitly transformational structures, i.e., codes 27 and 28; and the rest serve syntactic analyses, code 25, which is often combined with some complex technique.

Considering the developmental trends, a complex picture is encountered. There is only one clearly negative trend, pair 2–25—which by the way is counterevidence to the just preceding suggestion that codes 2 and 25 might serve complex morphology- and syntax-teaching functions. Under this assumption the pair should increase with development. But in accordance with the above argument, the pairs containing the most difficult items show increasing trends, pairs 24–24, 24–25, 24–27, and 24–28. As is evident from the correlation patterns of most of the other pairs, they indicate instances of net or classical suppression wherein the partial correlations are relatively low. No attempt to specify the partial correlations or to interpret the patterns will therefore be made.

Both the data presented in the last three tables and theoretical considerations require that a cautionary pause be inserted at this place and that the presumptions of the preceding sections be evaluated as to their justification. The results presented indicated for all three tables several consistently recurring code combinations in the pairs. But the same code combinations could also be encountered if the interactions were not structured at all and if only differential frequencies of occurrence of the individual items would lead to frequent chance cooccurrences between the more frequent single codes. In order to interpret the above pairs as real interactional patterns, it is required that the obtained frequencies of the pairs be contrasted with the expected frequencies, and that a criterion be established to evaluate the significance of the differences between the two values. This will be the task of the next section.

Real interactional patterns or chance cooccurrences of codes? To exhaustively and systematically evaluate and confirm the fact that the interactions between Eve and her mother are patterned, the observed frequencies of pairs have to be contrasted with the randomly expected cooccurrences. It was, however, deemed unnecessary to demonstrate statistically sequential dependencies in the case of Illocutionary Force codes, since it will barely be doubted that question-answer sequences, request-compliance sequences, and most of the other illocutionary doubles described are pragmatically and conversationally meaningful patterns. Since no instructional patterns have been explored previously and since they therefore will be less obvious, the task of contrasting observed and expected frequencies needs to be faced for the combinations of maternal techniques and Eve's learning strategies.

Two approaches could be chosen in the presentation of the pertinent data: The exact pairs presented in Tables 25 to 27 could be repeated in the following tables and could be evaluated as to their expected and observed frequencies. On the other hand, the clearest interactional structures could be presented in the following tables and the two sets of tables could be compared as to their overlap or lack of it in their pair members. The latter approach was chosen for the present presentation, since it is more informative. Any lack of overlap will be briefly commented upon in the discussion of each table.

Table 28 compares with Table 25 in that the child is in both the initiator of the sequences of utterances described. The structure of the table is largely self-explanatory if the footnotes are taken into consideration. In addition, the use of the z value was discussed in the method section. It suffices therefore to repeat that the z value does not strictly stand for probabilities, since the observations are not independent. However, the authors most versed in its use (Bakeman, 1978; Gottman & Bakeman, 1979) felt confident to employ a cutting point of two in the z values, i.e., around the value of 1.96 that signifies a p value of .05, in ascribing at least practical significance to the patterns. For the present tables, a large margin of safety was preferred, and only pairs with much higher z values are presented. In Table 28, the lower limit of the z value for inclusion of a pattern was chosen as 10.0. The patterns encountered in the table are therefore outstanding indeed. A brief comparison between observed and expected values shows this perhaps more convincingly than the standardized z values. Comparing Tables 25 and 28, it is seen that only three pairs of Table 25 are not found in Table 28. They are the doubles 29–24, 29–2, and 51–24. Their z values are 3.2, 5.7, and 2.3 respectively, so that they can

TABLE 28
Patterns of Strategies/Techniques Initiated by the Child and Completed by the Mother that Provide the Strongest Evidence for Interactional Structure

Pattern	n_{ij} Observed frequencies	e_{ij} Expected frequencies[a]	z[b]	$p_{j/i}$
29–29	197	62.6	24.8	.16
29–80	101	35.7	12.1	.08
51–2	100	33.7	16.9	.11
24–24	98	29.9	28.5	.18
51–80	86	25.6	15.4	.10
2–80	84	19.7	21.4	.12
25–2	79	32.4	12.3	.09
22–2	65	29.4	10.4	.08
51–51	65	24.5	10.3	.07
24–29	53	26.9	15.1	.10
50–80	48	11.5	20.6	.12
53–50	39	1.4	43.2	.20
24–1	39	9.8	12.2	.07

[a] $e_{ij} = N_2 \cdot n_i n_j / N_1^2$
[b] $z = \dfrac{n_{ij} - e_{ij}}{\sqrt{n_i p_j Q}}$

be quite confidently counted as established instructional patterns too.

Considering first the last four pairs in Table 28 that were not discussed in Table 25, the patterns are instructionally quite meaningful in at least three of the four doubles. The 50–80 pattern reflects the fact that Eve often can expect a conditioned reward when she utters a label. That the actual contingencies are higher than the transitional probability of .12 suggests will be demonstrated in a subsequent section. Highly impressive is the contrast between expected and observed frequencies in the case of the double 53–50. Expressed in words: If the child asks for a label, code 53, the chances are high that it will be supplied immediately. The transitional probability of code 50 following Eve's code 53 is .20, a very high probability if the large number of categories and therefore the large number of possible sequences are considered. That the transitional probability is not higher is due to the fact that the mother has other options to respond with when Eve asks for a label. Most impressive were those instances when the mother 'reflected the question back' to Eve—since she knew supposedly that Eve should be familiar with the label—a technique captured by the Illocutionary Force code 9. In these instances, Eve could often provide the label herself, demonstrating thereby that her mother had an astonishingly good knowledge of Eve's vocabulary repertoire.

It might be helpful to briefly consider the transitional probabilities given in the rightmost column of Tables 28 to 30. The obtained values have to be compared with the random probability of a specific response following any utterance of the child. Since approximately 80 categories were employed for mother and child together, and since each conversation partner could produce several utterances in a row which were coded as strategies or techniques, the random transitional probability from one utterance to the next is approximately 1:80 or .0125. Compared to this random or expected transitional probability, the observed ones are between 5 and 22 times as high.

Returning specifically to Table 28 and considering the pair 24–1, a psychologically meaningful principle can be again recognized. That the mother would respond with an identical imitation, code 1, when the child managed to correctly employ a bound morpheme, code 24, is instructionally useful, since it provides an instance of rehearsal of an item, i.e., a bound morpheme, in which Eve was still quite weak during the period under study. Only the fourth new double, 24–29, Eve's perseveration of a morpheme being followed by the mother's perseveration of a vocabulary item, does not immediately appear instructionally meaningful. It could even be argued that the mother might thereby overtax the information processing capacity of Eve. An understanding of this pattern will have to be sought either from the analysis of longer chains of interactions or from qualitative studies of patterns, i.e., of the actual linguistic items employed in them.

Since all the other pairs in Table 28 have already been encountered and touched upon in connection with Table 25, any repetition would be redundant. Only the overall import of the results in Table 28 might deserve specification: The pairs are not only common in regard to their frequencies, the maternal techniques are also quite predictable. The child can expect one of three response patterns from her mother: When Eve says something linguistically informative/important, her mother will repeat it. When Eve makes a linguistic advance, she will be rewarded for it, code 80. Often reward and repetition are combined, as the subsequent analysis of longer chains will show. Finally and most impressive, if Eve asks for linguistic information, code 53, the chances are high the mother will provide it immediately. The later analysis of longer chains of interaction would show that Eve has almost complete assurance that the information will be provided, either immediately or after testing or repair sequences.

In Table 29 are presented those pairs of utterances which were initiated by the mother and responded to by the child. The sequence is therefore mother's technique—Eve's strategy. Table 29 is to be compared with Table 26 in order to evaluate whether the pairs presented there were real interactional patterns or mere random cooccurrences. In contrast to the comparison between the Tables 25 and 28, for which the categories overlapped almost completely, there is only minimal overlap between the Tables 26 and 29. Only the patterns 29–29 and 51–2 reappear in Table 29 with high z values.

TABLE 29
Patterns of Techniques/Strategies Initiated by the Mother and Responded to by the Child that Provide the Strongest Evidence for Interactional Structure

Pattern	n_{ij} Observed frequencies	e_{ij} Expected frequencies[a]	z^b	$p_{j/i}$
29–29	160	62.6	15.5	.11
51–2	58	18.9	11.3	.07
61–51	56	17.8	15.0	.10
27–51	54	10.1	30.8	.17
53–50	45	2.3	56.7	.27
54–51	44	4.8	58.9	.28
61–23	43	12.2	12.1	.07
60–20	42	3.6	38.0	.19
61–22	41	15.5	10.0	.07
61–29	40	14.5	10.1	.07

$^a e_{ij} = N_2 \cdot n_i n_j / N_1^2$

$^b z = \dfrac{n_{ij} - e_{ij}}{\sqrt{n_i p_j Q}}$

Those two patterns are certainly of great importance for language learning in that the first one deals most clearly with vocabulary acquisition and the latter with syntax learning. Eve has obviously already established a quite predictable strategy; the transitional probabilities are .11 and .07, respectively, for the most basic tasks of language acquisition. The strategy is: Repeat the model in its most important aspects. In contrast, the doubles in Table 26 containing a code 24, morpheme perseveration, have z values ranging only from 2.7 to 8.5, and the same range of values applies for the pairs beginning with more complex maternal techniques such as 25 and 27. They are therefore real patterns, even if less predictable. Only the pair 25–29 in Table 26 obtains a z value of less than two, i.e., 1.5, and can therefore not be labelled a response pattern in a statistical sense. The z and p values in Table 29 demonstrate, however, that Eve has developed highly predictable strategies in coping with specific types of input: z values in the thirties and fifties combined with transitional probabilities in the tens and twenties are evidence for such strong patterns. Impressively, the three strongest patterns, 54–51, 53–50, and 60–20, appear in those instances where the maternal technique is expressed in the illocutionary form of a question. It can here again be seen that Eve has learned quite well that questions require an adequate answer and that she follows this principle quite consistently. Four of the other patterns begin with technique 61, which also has almost always the illocutionary force of a question when employed by Eve's mother. Only the pattern 27–51 is not immediately understandable and requires further exploration.

The comparison of Tables 29 and 26 can now be summarized briefly: Eve has learned the question-answer pattern well, and if her mother formulates her teaching techniques in question form she can expect quite reliably an adequate answer. Many of the conversationally less obvious maternal techniques that were found in Table 26, while having a tendency to elicite a specific response with a frequency clearly above chance, do, however, not very consistently elicit one specific strategy from Eve. Whether this pattern suggests flexibility in learning strategies or, more often, random unpredictability will have to be explored in qualitative analyses.

Table 30 is to be compared with Table 27 and deals like it with pairs of utterances produced by the mother in immediate succession. It raises very interesting questions in regard to those patterns of the mother presented in Table 27. As seen from the comparison, the first six patterns in both tables are identical and they have considerable z values and transitional probabilities. These patterns, with the exception of pattern 28–25, can be summarized in one single rule that the mother follows: If the first intervention was not successful, repeat the same technique. The last five pairs in Table 27 obtain z values of between .3 and 1.7 and are therefore not patterns in the strict sense. They are merely due to the fact that the mother is prone to frequently use the techniques composing them. It remains to be seen whether this statistical lack of significance is to be interpreted as instructional flexibility or just

TABLE 30
Patterns of Techniques Both Produced by the Mother
that Provide the Strongest Evidence
for Interactional Structure

Pattern	n_{ij} Observed frequencies	e_{ij} Expected frequencies[a]	z^{b}	$p_{j/i}$
24–24	145	89.6	7.0	.09
29–29	130	73.0	6.3	.09
25–25	114	61.7	5.8	.09
27–27	102	64.3	6.4	.07
28–28	96	39.5	12.1	.09
28–25	86	49.4	7.8	.08
80–2	68	31.6	10.0	.08
80–29	64	41.6	6.1	.08
2–80	63	31.1	6.5	.06
51–27	60	37.3	6.6	.08
51–51	53	21.6	9.1	.07
81–28	36	7.9	30.5	.17

[a] $e_{ij} = N_2 \cdot n_i n_j / N_1^2$

[b] $z = \dfrac{n_{ij} - e_{ij}}{\sqrt{n_i p_j Q}}$

randomness, and whether Eve benefits from this input even if it is not above random expectation.

Continuing with the remaining patterns in Table 30, three principles can be seen. For the pattern 51–51, the above formulated principle holds: continue with the same technique. 51–27 could be a syntactically very instructional pattern, since, first, with the code 51, an environmental structure is mapped upon a linguistic structure to assure semantic obviousness, and then the child is shown how this linguistic structure can be varied, code 27, without a meaning change. Two types of redundancy are thereby utilized by the mother: situational and linguistic/contextual redundancy. The three patterns containing 80, conditioned reward, will be discussed below, when this controversial topic is explored in detail, and shall therefore be omitted at present. There remains only the quite rare but highly structured pattern of 81–28, feedback informing Eve that her linguistic utterance was not acceptable being followed by optional transformations. It is suspected that it is somewhat of an artifact of the illocutionary pattern that followed a response providing negative feedback with a question; but it needs further exploration.

Stability of patterns versus versatility of teaching/learning methods. The discussion of the various pairs and patterns of techniques and strategies that began with Table 22 could have lead to the impression of great stability and even rigidity in the response tendencies of both partners of the interactions. Tables 29 and 30 already have provided considerable evidence that suggested that even frequent pairs could be due to random cooccurrences of items and that even strongly patterned pairs, that is pairs with high z values, have transitional probabilities of only around .10 to .20. If a specific subsequent item follows only once in five to ten instances of the preceding item, the question certainly arises what the second items of the pair are in the other four or nine instances. The thereby suggested instructional and learning versatility shall now be considered in more detail.

Several topics are of considerable interest in the present context. In accordance with the emphasis of the study, the mother's versatility in responding to the child's language trials is of primary importance. Versatility can be defined in two ways: The mother might either employ a variety of techniques in responding to one and the same strategy of Eve, or she might use a single technique flexibly in responding to several different strategies of the child. Reward, for example, could follow vocabulary mastery as well as advances in syntactic or morphological skills. Since the mother's techniques are predominantly of interest in so far as they have an impact upon Eve's language performance, the strategies of Eve have to be explored in their variety too. Finally, "repair sequences," chosen by the mother if a single intervention of hers does not lead immediately to the desired result, might also be composed flexibly and in a versatile manner.

Before the content of specific figures can be discussed, a few general remarks pertaining to the next four figures might be helpful. In Figures 1, 3, and 4 one single antecedent or criterion strategy/technique is juxtaposed with the strategies/techniques that follow it. In Figure 2, the single maternal techniques of the subsets follow a wide variety of Eve's strategies. The sections of the figures containing the various alternative responses, or the antecedents in Figure 2, consist of three columns each. The first specifies the code; the second, headed by a F_0, the observed frequencies; and the third, headed by a F_e, the expected frequencies. The lowest observed frequency in each subset gives the cutting line below which pairs were not included. A comparison of observed and expected frequencies makes it possible to differentiate whether the preceding strategy/technique either enhances the probability of the subsequent one to follow it, diminishes this probability, or leaves it unaffected. Although all three types of sequences are commonly found in the subsequent figures, the main attention will be paid to those antecedent behaviors that enhance the probability of the subsequent ones to occur. A few remarks about the possible reasons for clear inhibiting effects will be encountered, but it is fully admitted that these remarks represent very preliminary hypotheses. Finally it will be seen that, repeatedly, pairs are interpreted as to their possible instructional effects even if they do not consist of structured sequences in the statistical sense that their frequence of cooccurrence clearly surpasses that expected from random probabilities. This is based upon the fact that highly interesting and complex relationships between tightness of interactional contingencies and instructional value are expected. Very rare and therefore outstanding responses could certainly have—and do have in information-theory terms—a high information value. On the other hand, the mother or child might employ a technique/strategy in a temporal rhythm that is most conducive to learning and is quite independent of the immediately preceding strategies/techniques. Suggestive evidence for such temporal rhythms have been noticed in relation to the provision and rehearsal of new vocabulary items. Complete absence of first-order transitional dependencies could be combined with patterns of profound importance for the teaching and learning of language. Higher order Markov chain analyses or multi-lag sequential analyses will have to be performed to explore these patterns.

Figure 1 encompasses five different subsets of occasion for the flexible responding of the mother. Each subset will be briefly discussed. In subset (a), code 29 represents Eve's vocabulary acquisition strategy, subset (b) deals with Eve's bound-morpheme rehearsal, code 24, and the other subsets pertain mainly to different aspects of syntax mastery, codes 2, 25, and 51. These last three codes stand, however, for contrasting strategies of Eve: Code 51 denotes mainly spontaneous syntactic construction; code 2 represents instances of responsive syntax rehearsal after a maternal model, and code 25 indicates again a spontaneous restructuring of a sentence. Only the more frequent patterns are included in the subsets of Figure 1, so that even the last ones in the rank order occur on the average at least once per hour of recording. That the mother's reactions to Eve's strategies are absolutely not rigid is quite obvious from these first five figures. Another trait common to four of the five sets shown in Figure 1 is that the maternal code 80, conditioned reinforcement, appears with one exception either in first or second place of the frequency rank orders. That is, in spite of her flexibility, the mother makes certain in a large percentage of the child's trials to provide positive feedback. It will be seen from Table 31 that the frequency of positive reinforcement encountered in these figures is certainly an underestimation. Since the mother attaches her word of praise almost randomly either to the beginning or the end of her contentive response, the presentation of child-mother utterance pairs of necessity omits around half the instances of conditioned positive reinforcement that follow a specific strategy of the child.

In the subsets (a), (c), (d), and (e) of Figure 1, a few further common points shall be selected for discussion: The high frequency of the maternal code 2, which involves largely the addition of minor free and bound morphemes, is quite obvious. Since all maternal codes between 20 and 26 signify maternal self-repetition, the pertinent pairs suggest a more complex interactional structure: the mother employed a technique, the child, as shown in one of the codes on the left hand of the figures, utilized the maternal

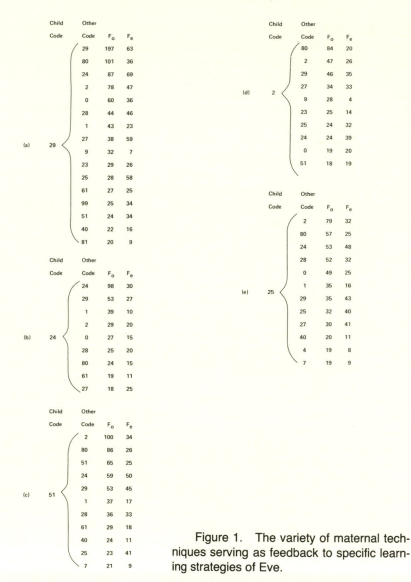

Figure 1.   The variety of maternal techniques serving as feedback to specific learning strategies of Eve.

input, and now the mother, as shown on the right-hand side, rehearses, expands, or varies her own input in a third step of the instructional chain. Code 9 in the sets (a) and (d) signifies a very similar procedure. Overt corrections, codes 40 or 81, are certainly not absent—see subsets (a), (c), and (e)—but they appear invariably towards the end of the frequency rank order. In the case where Eve has shown by means of her reduced imitation, code 2, that she has probably exerted her processing capacities to the maximum limit, these overt corrections do not appear under the more frequent patterns. The same

applies to subset (b), bound-morpheme rehearsal, wherein Eve is still relatively weak. Finally, the quite consistent appearance of transformations in
the maternal responses, in the form of codes 27 and 28, deserves mentioning,
since it represents the principle of rehearsal with variation which has been
shown in education and psychology to be effective for teaching and learning.

The maternal responses following the child's code 24 are somewhat different, at least as far as the most frequent items are concerned. Three of the
four most frequent maternal responses, i.e., 24, 1, and 2, indicate that the
mother emphasizes direct repetition of the morpheme the child attempted.
The code 29 probably indicates that not only the morpheme but also the exact
word was often repeated. To be certain about this, the actual utterance chains
have to be rechecked, however. Repetition, though in a transformed and
therefore more complex form, is also suggested by the codes 28 and 27. With
the exception of code 80, reward, and the codes 0 and 61 whose meaning is
not clear, the emphasis certainly seems to lie upon immediate repetition
when the child produces a bound morpheme. Knowing that Eve is still
struggling very much with bound morphemes, these maternal response patterns suggest massed training that has been shown to be so effective in the initial stages of learning. Such suggestions of massed initial training that is then
gradually replaced by more spaced rehearsal have been repeatedly encountered in the study of the transcripts. To demonstrate them, different approaches to data analysis are required that will be presented in a subsequent
report.

Figure 2 with its five subsets presents a different perspective upon maternal flexibility, namely how flexibly she employs one specific technique to
respond to a variety of learning strategies of the child. Subset (a), pertaining
to the maternal use of conditioned reward, code 80, barely needs comment.
Clear vocabulary exercises, codes 29 and 50, are as equally rewarded as the
strategies more emphasizing syntax, 51, 2, 25, 22, 27, 23. All of these and also
codes 9 and 20 could, of course, involve vocabulary and bound morphemes
too. The low frequency of reward for bound morphemes, which was also
found in Figure 1, together with the evidence from the transcripts about
Eve's low level of bound-morpheme competency, might suggest that the
mother had the feeling it was too early to emphasize bound-morpheme suc-
cess. Since she did not neglect bound-morpheme rehearsal, as demonstrated
above, it might also be the case that bound-morpheme learning is not often
rewarded by those utterance forms coded as 80. Since a bound morpheme is a
very minor constituent of an utterance, simple praise by the mother would
probably not clearly indicate for the child that she intended to reward the
production of this bound morpheme. Other feedback techniques might be required to convey this message.

When discussing maternal rewards, it might deserve reemphasizing that
the maternal codes 2 and 1 in subsets (b) and (c), and any accepting repetition
by the adult of the child's utterance, entail an aspect of positive reinforcement

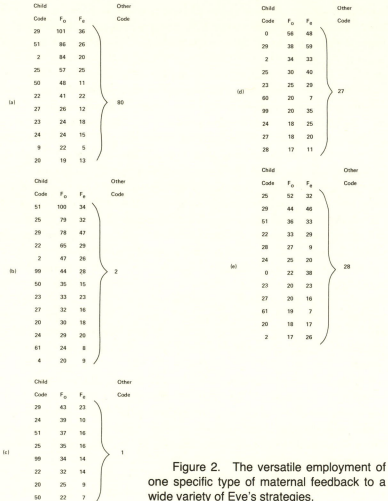

Figure 2. The versatile employment of one specific type of maternal feedback to a wide variety of Eve's strategies.

too. In imitating the child's utterance in identical or even a changed form, the adult conveys the message to the child that her formulation was "acceptable," that is, largely correct. This consideration also entails a possibility as to how mothers could differentially reward bound-morpheme production by the child. Since mothers generally employ exaggerated intonation, as found by many previous investigators, maternal imitation of the bound morpheme with added intonation might be a most conducive technique to inform the child about the item of emphasis and to reward her at the same time. This possibility would have to be evaluated on the basis of actual tape recordings. Besides this reward aspect, techniques 2 and 1 also have a corrective function. This correction is entailed by the definition of technique 2, i.e., expanding imitation, and it is concealed by the label for technique 1, "identical imitation." Code 1 often involves phonetic corrections which could not be exhaustively analyzed on the basis of mere transcripts. The context for these corrections is certainly optimal. Eve had conveyed the message before and the meaning of it is therefore fully established. Since the mother imitates all the major message elements, minimal processing for the larger syntactic pattern and the contentive aspects is required. Eve can therefore fully attend to the finer items of improvement the mother offers. The analyses of triple and longer chains of interactions will provide the evidence how well—and sometimes not so well—Eve utilizes this input. The left sides of subsets (b) and (c) in Figure 2 suggest that the mother employs imitation predominantly for the rehearsal of syntactic patterns, though vocabulary, codes 29 and 50, and bound morphemes, code 24, are imitated by Eve's mother too.

Subsets (d) and (e) contrast with the preceding three subsets in that the maternal feedback is more demanding on the information processing capacities of the child. The mother transforms some preceding utterance and the child has to analyze the new pattern. In the case of 0–27, Figure 2, (d), this might be a repair sequence after the communication had broken down. The mother might try to reformulate an utterance so as to help the child to comprehend it. Rehearsed vocabulary items, code 29, are often presented in transformed sentence frames, a method that helps clarify their syntactic functions. A brief glance at a few of the specific patterns might suggest the sophistication of the teaching/learning sequences. In the case of the child's code 2, a maternal model has just been utilized and the mother shows now how this model can be transformed. In the case of the child's code 25, Eve has just experimented with constituent replacement in one of her own preceding utterances and the mother adds again transformations to the constituent replacement attempted by Eve. Transformational chains, i.e., child 27 or 28 followed by maternal 27 or 28, are not unknown and should provide almost optimal opportunities for the learning of transformations.

Much instructional sophistication and impact has been assumed in interpreting the above data, but neither has been demonstrated. Although it will not be possible to fully demonstrate this instructional impact in the present study, at least some evidence for or against it needs to be provided. This will be attempted in Figure 3 with its seven subsets of patterns that pertain to those maternal instructional techniques that have been mostly emphasized in the above sections. Codes pertaining to reward and corrections will be discussed separately in the next section.

A brief comparative glance over the seven subsets will reveal an astonishing fact. Up to now the instructional skill of the mother was emphasized and it was taken for granted that her linguistic input was well adapted to Eve's capacities. Figure 3 serves now a corrective function in that it shows that, for most of the subsets, a 0 code in the child's column is first or second in frequen-

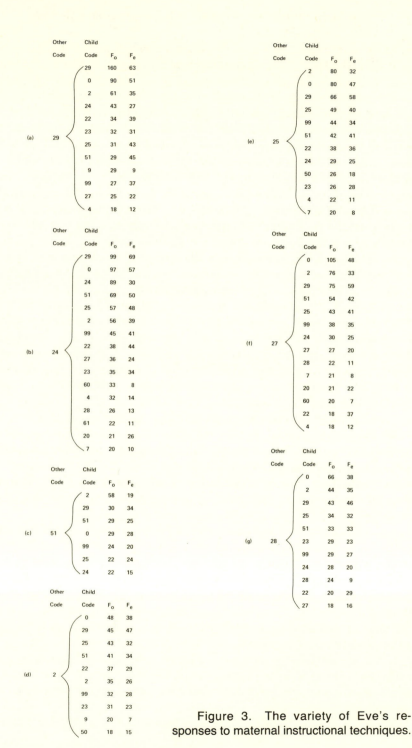

Figure 3. The variety of Eve's responses to maternal instructional techniques.

cy. Whereas this zero code directly indicates an inaudible utterance on the tape or a simple *yes* response given by Eve, it suggests more indirectly that Eve's linguistic processing capacity was overtaxed, which led to a partial breakdown in her language production. Having once attended to Eve's limited processing capacities, a further pattern demonstrates the same and also shows how Eve copes with this limitation. With quite minor exceptions, the seven subsets exhibit common tendencies of Eve comprising only few alternatives in the highest ranks: (a) Eve either repeats the same code that the mother modeled, that is 29–29, 24–24, 25–25, 51–51; (b) the emphasis might mainly lie upon repeating a new or rare word, code 29; or (c) she imitates the mother's model in a simplified form, code 2. Those strategies, plus the code 0, are generally the first ones in the seven subsets.

Those standard response strategies of Eve certainly remind the psychologist of the extended research concerning habit hierarchies and of how, in stressful situations, habits of greatest strength and minimal complexity tend to take over. Panic is the most extreme case of this; and Eve's zero code might resemble such a "minimal" reaction. But luckily for Eve and her mother, these simplistic reactions do not exhaust the response repertoire of Eve. Below these most frequent response categories follow in the rank order other 20-codes which suggest that Eve was able in many cases to actively and immediately incorporate the maternal input into her own preceding sentences by changing the latter. These codes include the more complex ones, namely 22, 24, 25, 27, and 28. If Eve employs imitation of her mother's model, it is also often creative imitation involving considerable changes, i.e., codes 4, 7, and 9. The above exhibited "primitive" response tendencies are therefore counterbalanced by several more advanced ones. Qualitative analyses of triple sequences of the type Mother-Child-Child would show that the "simplistic" responses of reduced imitation, vocabulary perseveration, and straight imitation of the technique are only stop-gap measures. Immediately following this "simplistic response," Eve often incorporates the maternal model into a more complex learning strategy, showing thereby that the maternal model was not absolutely above her capacities but that she only needed a few extra seconds of processing time to master it constructively. But this large and complex topic pertaining to the child's learning strategies had to be excluded from consideration here in order to keep the amount of information within manageable bounds.

Since Eve often seems to struggle with the complex incoming linguistic information, the question of what the mother does when Eve cannot immediately master her input needs to be again dealt with. Pairs of successive maternal utterances will be studied again, but this time in contrast to table 27 with an emphasis upon maternal flexibility. Figure 4 with its seven subsets provides this information.

It is probably not a coincidence that all the maternal successive pairs of

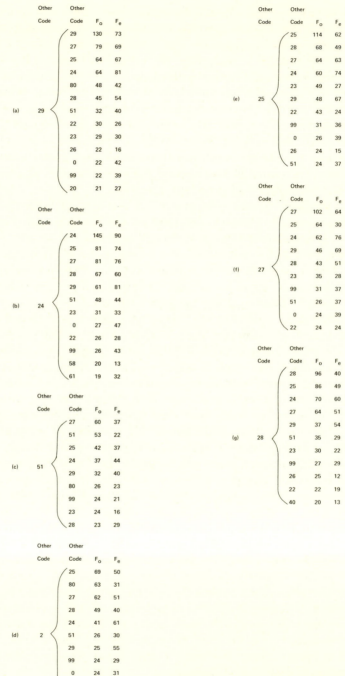

Figure 4.   Maternal versatility in successive techniques.

techniques in Table 27 and 30 and again here in Figure 4 deal with syntactic and morphological aspects. From the transcripts of Eve's speech, it is evident that she is still struggling with many aspects of these two language domains, whereas, as was suggested, vocabulary perseveration is almost an easy escape response. The mother's predominant tendency when Eve encounters processing problems can also be summarized as consisting of a few principles. (a) If a technique does not immediately produce results, repeat it, i.e., patterns 24–24, 29–29, 25–25, 27–27, 28–28, 51–51. This is the most common tendency and was also discussed in connection with Table 30. (b) If simple repetition of the initial code is impossible by definition, as in the case of code 2, or if it is inadvisable, the second most prevalent alternative is to repeat the preceding syntactic structure but to replace some constituents by others, code 25. Inspection of the actual utterance sequences indicates that this replacement results mostly in an easier message, since a more familiar and simpler word is substituted for those constituents that were less familiar to the child. In operational terms: More commonly encountered items replace less common ones. Alternative (c) as encountered in the code 27 closely rivals alternative (b) in frequency. The code 27 encompasses many aspects of linguistic transformations and it is therefore an over-simplification to call its employment "one alternative." A common form employed by Eve's mother was the rephrasing of a full-verb sentence with a copula sentence, followed by other simplified sentences. An example of this technique would be: Mother's first utterance: "Look at the hopping bunny rabbit." Followed by: "This is a bunny rabbit. He is hopping." The maternal techniques of 25 and 27 do not only occupy similar places in the rank orders of the subsets, they are also procedurally closely equivalent: with technique 25, the syntax remains the same and some constituents are changed, whereas with technique 27, the meaning remains the same and the syntax is changed.

The bases for the following techniques might be less obvious from a mere inspection of Figure 4: The frequent appearance of code 24, i.e., morpheme perseveration, might even appear counterintuitive. Eve's previously emphasized difficulties in morpheme learning might suggest this. If, however, the fact is considered that code 24 indicates morpheme perseveration, i.e., an exact repetition of something already present in a preceding utterance, then it also entails a lowering of the information processing load. Similarly, the code 28, optional transformations, is defined by retention of highly similar meanings, which involves also the retention of most vocabulary items, combined with syntactic changes. Redundancy is certainly involved in such instances too. Whereas code 23, break-down sequences, makes sense in cases of information overload, the code 22, build-up sequences, appears counterintuitive. The study of longer sequences of maternal utterances can explain this result. It shows, namely, that codes 22, 23, and 25 are common elements of repair sequences. A preliminary impression indicates that their sequential arrangement might be quite arbitrary and that individual codes are optional. Together they seem to help the child to analyze syntactic constructions that proved difficult at first encounter.

In summary: The mother relies upon redundancies and minor modifications in her input to give Eve the chance of repeated exposure for information processing purposes, and she performs replacements, deletions, and additions of major constituents, which makes the underlying syntactic structure more conspicuous. As the mother uses linguistic redundancy when she repeats verbal elements and structures, so she utilizes situational redundancy when she employs the technique 51, structural syntactic mapping.

With these few patterns, most regularities encountered in the subsets of Figure 4 are described. The less common appearance of the code 26, replacement sequence of minor elements, follows the same principle as code 25. Some cases of correction and questioning would probably appear meaningful when studied specifically in the transcripts. Though the code of 99, Other, appears quite frequently, its observed frequency is consistently lower than the frequency expected from random probabilities and it does therefore not reflect an instructional pattern.

The special topics of reward, correction, and negative feedback. These topics have been the subject of continued controversy and they represent to a large degree the touchstone for the various theoretical approaches: corrections for cognitive hypothesis–testing interpretations; and rewards and negative feedback for behavioristic ones. In the present study, the maternal technique coded 80 entails many features of conditioned reward as defined by the behaviorists, the technique coded 40 represents the most obvious form of maternal correction, and technique 81 comes as close as possible to conditioned punishment. Doubles that contain either of these codes will be explored in the next three tables. First, maternal reward, code 80, for the child's successful utterances or at least for her attempts to communicate linguistically, will be discussed.

It will be remembered that maternal praise in the form of the words "good," "yes," "well said," etc. were coded as 80. That is, technique 80 represents maternal praise for linguistic performance. Little argument should exist that maternal praise is something most normal children desire, and that they experience its provision as something positive. Whereas technique 80 presents a clear case of conditioned reward, it is not implied that other forms of maternal reward were not encountered. It has been argued that maternal imitation can have strong reward aspects, and all the non-verbal signals of reward such as smiles, hugs, etc., and the paralinguistic phenomena such as tone of voice, have to be considered, though they could not be included in the present analysis.

It has been mentioned that Eve's mother inserted her words of praise in a seemingly arbitrary manner either before or after a pertinent content utterance of hers. Table 31 presents therefore those pairs of maternal utterances that immediately succeeded themselves and that contained a form of praise in either position. The pairs of utterances are ordered in accordance with their frequency of appearance in the corpus from the most frequent pair to that which appeared at least ten times in the twenty hours analyzed. The general design of the tables will be obvious by now and only selected points need to be discussed in the text. First, the overall frequency of the pairs containing the code 80 is of interest. Table 20 provided the information that a total of 474 instances of the code 80 were encountered in the 20 hours analyzed, which

TABLE 31

Patterns of Successive Maternal Utterances in which She Employs Conditioned Positive Reinforcement

Pattern	Observed frequencies, n_{ij}	Expected frequencies, e_{ij}[a]	z[b]
80–2	68	31	8.89
80–29	64	42	4.64
2–80	63	31	7.64
80–24	57	24	6.60
29–80	48	42	1.24
80–27	39	39	0
80–25	38	38	0
80–51	37	23	3.97
1–80	27	15	4.10
80–23	27	17	3.21
51–80	26	23	0.84
80–6	20	12	3.13
80–1	17	15	0.69
80–40	17	10	2.83
80–22	15	15	0
24–80	15	46	−6.08
80–28	15	31	−3.89
9–80	15	5	5.95
80–4	13	7	2.91
80–58	12	7	2.58
80–61	12	17	−1.64
40–80	12	10	0.82
23–80	11	17	−1.94
6–80	11	12	−0.39
80–99	10	22	−3.40

[a] $e_{ij} = N_2 n_i n_j / N_1^2$

[b] $z = \dfrac{n_{ij} - e_{ij}}{\sqrt{n_i p_j Q}}$

suggests that Eve heard a word of praise almost every second minute. The contrast between the total of observed pairs in Table 31, which is 689, and the number 474 results from the fact that maternal praise is often interspersed between two other utterances of hers. In these latter cases, it was double-counted in Table 31. The numerical relationships of 689 versus 474, combined with the fact that only the more frequent pairs were counted, indicates that in around 50% of maternal reward this reward is sandwiched in between two other utterances of the mother. Interesting combinations of reward plus correction and other forms of information provision are therefore possible and await exploring. Table 31 suggests a function of the code 80 besides that of reward, that of camouflage or dissimulation of the negative flavor of corrective feedback. When encountering these patterns, the writer was often reminded of Mary Poppins' song: "A little bit of sugar helps the medicine go down." Considering the difference between the linguistic level of the mother and that of the child, and the fact that almost every maternal utterance is so much more accomplished than the child's, it can be estimated how much "medicine" the child has to cope with. In the present system of analysis, most imitation techniques, technique 40 and 51, as well as many of the instances when one of the 20-codes was chosen, contained corrections. Code 81 conveyed most obviously this negative evaluation. The partially completed qualitative analyses suggest that the twenty hours analyzed entail many hundreds of instances of correction—in the wider meaning of the word—and that a considerable dose of "sugar" might be required so as not to discourage Eve. Basically, the message the mother often conveys, since she cannot avoid improving and correcting Eve's linguistic output, is: "Yes, you have done it well—but it certainly can be improved upon in . . . ." The second part of this message may be more or less emphasized, but it is entailed in every feedback that is more accomplished than the child's preceding utterance. Since it can and will be shown that the corrective force of the feedback often does not escape the child, the terms "camouflage" or "dissimulation" might be less apt than "counterbalancing" or "consolation." In an interesting twist of methodology, clearly positive evaluations are combined with clearly evident corrections.

Table 31 suggests, however, and a close study of triples could prove it, that the reward function is quite often dominant when the mother employs strategy 80. Those doubles that contain a code 29 or 51 were largely preceded by the equivalent child strategy, and the mother says therefore in principle: "Good; exactly as you said it." The same message is conveyed by the mother through the double 80–1 or 1–80. 80–2 and 2–80 can have almost the same function and so do 80–24 or 24–80 if they are preceded by Eve's 24. Although the temptation was great to add a table of triples to demonstrate these patterns, it was resisted since much of the pertinent information can be found in Figures 5 and 6, which presently follow, and is even clearer in the lefthand side of Table 34.

Comparing these phenomena of reinforcement that are intermixed and often integrally combined with corrections, a discussion of intrinsic versus extrinsic motivation and of the "optimal level of discrepancy" (Hunt, 1965) would be called for. But this would lead too far off the main theme and it could not be adequately dealt with within the confines of this study. Moerk (1977b) has surveyed most extensively these questions of motivation, and he has (Moerk, 1976b, 1978) provided some preliminary evidence pertaining to these topics. Since so much emphasis has been placed upon the corrective aspect of maternal feedback, a closer study of it is more urgently required. Table 32 provides some pertinent evidence.

Only the corrective and negative feedback provided by the mother, coded 40 and 81, has been summarized, since the maternal code of 41, challenge, was very rarely encountered. Altogether there were 209 instances of the code 40 and 122 instances of the code 81 in the verbal behavior of the mother. Of the pairs occurring with a frequency of three or more, 195 contained the code 40 and 105 the code 81, as seen in Table 32. The evidence is quite unequivocal as to which strategy types of Eve are responded to by her mother with the technique coded 40. Whereas the code 29, the child's attempt at vocabulary rehearsal, appears high up in the frequency rank order, the overwhelming majority of the child's strategies fall into the code range of the twenties that pertain to syntactic exercises. The code 51 entails, by definition, syntactic constructions also, though it is easily possible that labeling errors might be corrected by the mother too. Adding up the frequencies for the pairs beginning with the codes 51 and all twenties, with the exception of 29, a subtotal of 121 instances is attained in which syntactic correction by means of the code 40 is highly likely, though it would have to be demonstrated for each individual case. To this need probably to be added the instances of code 40 following the subsets of imitation, coded 4 and 7, a subtotal of 15, and the three instances of 40 following the code 58, adverbial clauses. This would result in approximately 140 instances wherein contrasting syntactic correction is highly likely. Since the codes 29, 50, and 56 were mainly employed for the coding of some forms of vocabulary training, this subtotal of around 30 pairs should represent an estimate of vocabulary correction in the form of code 40. The around twenty instances in which 24 and 2 are followed by 40 suggest how rarely obvious correction is employed for bound-morpheme teaching.

The patterns containing as second element the code 81 are mainly identical to those containing 40 as second element. They suggest mainly feedback after syntactic mistakes intermixed with some vocabulary correction and only very few instances of bound-morpheme correction. Obvious corrections as summarized in Table 31 are much less frequent than rewards; they are, however, certainly not absent from maternal feedback.

A last question deserves brief scrutiny before a general conclusion can be drawn about obvious corrective and even negative feedback provided by the

TABLE 32

Patterns of Child - Mother Sequences in which the Mother Provides
Corrective and Negative Feedback

Pattern	Observed freq., n_{ij}	Expected freq., e_{ij}^a	z^b	Pattern	Observed freq., n_{ij}	Expected freq., e_{ij}^a	z^b
51–40	24	11	4.96	29–81	20	9	4.84
29–40	22	16	2.08	25–81	14	6	3.95
25–40	20	11	3.61	22–81	10	6	2.39
22–40	20	10	4.23	51–81	10	7	1.79
24–40	13	7	3.13	28–81	7	2	5.31
27–40	12	5	3.71	50–81	7	3	3.17
4–40	10	3	3.83	20–81	7	4	1.86
28–40	9	3	4.51	24–81	7	4	1.46
23–40	9	8	0.61	2–81	6	5	0.52
2–40	9	9	0.00	23–81	4	5	−0.32
99–40	6	9	−1.42	1–81	4	1	3.18
21–40	6	3	2.29	4–81	3	2	1.21
50–40	6	5	0.58	40–81	3	1	4.31
7–40	5	2	2.48	58–81	3	1	3.77
20–40	5	6	−0.54				
60–40	5	2	3.11				
61–40	5	3	2.07				
56–40	3	1	2.92				
26–40	3	2	0.51				
58–40	3	1	2.20				

$^a e_{ij} = N_2 n_i n_j / N_1^2$

$^b z = \dfrac{n_{ij} - e_{ij}}{\sqrt{n_{ij} p_j Q}}$

mother. If the mother feels the need to provide this strong and obvious form of critical feedback, does she do anything to make it a constructive learning experience? Table 33 contains a few suggestions pertaining to this question.

Table 33 summarizes all those maternal utterance pairs in which the codes 40 and 81 appeared. Those pairs containing the code 40 will be discussed first. The most frequent pair, 40–24, entails some surprise if compared with the results of the previous tables. Whereas evidence in Table 32 had suggested that Eve was not yet ready for bound-morpheme instruction and that her mother did not correct omissions of bound morphemes, the present pair suggests that more of the 40s of the mother might have entailed bound-morpheme corrections and that the mother thought it worthwhile to follow up this morpheme correction with a 24. The strong criticism/correction represented by the doubles 81–40 and 40–81, $N = 30$, is almost completely balanced by attempts to camouflage the correcting force of the code 40 in the doubles 40–80 and 80–40, $N = 29$. A double contrasting correction, 40–40, appears 20 times in the 20 hours analyzed, a frequency considerably higher than the expected one, which is 5 instances, but it hardly can affect the emotional climate of the interactions. Generally, it is of interest that only two strong patterns, i.e., 81–40 and 40–40, as shown by the z values, appear in connection with the code 40. Maternal contrastive correction seems therefore not to be dependent upon the mother's own immediately preceding utterance nor does it strongly determine the type of the following technique employed. Generally, her contrasting correction is mostly paired with a technique emphasizing syntactic teaching, as indicated by the frequent appearance of the 20 codes.

Similar principles hold for the pairs containing the code 81. Only the first three pairs, 81–28, 81–81, and 81–40 show high z values. The pair 81–40 is identical to that in the left section of Table 33, 81–81 is equivalent to 40–40, and the most frequent pattern, 81–28, is probably due to illocutionary dynamics: The mother follows a "no" with a question. Equally as 40, 81 is mostly combined with a syntax exercising technique of the mother.

A brief general review of the topic of correction and negative feedback seems now to be called for, since even the existence of these two maternal techniques has often been vigorously denied. It was pointed out in a previous section that the relationship of obviously positive to obviously negative feedback as indicated by the codes 80 versus 81 was 474 to 122. The relationship of the quite obvious correction, code 40, to the codes for various imitational forms, the codes from 1 to 9, which indicates mainly acceptance of the child's utterances, was 209 to around 1600. As expounded above, imitations might entail in themselves both positive and negative feedback aspects, so that this proportion has to be interpreted with some caution. Since, in the immediately preceding sections, the approximately 300 pairs of utterances that contained either 40 or 81 were stressed, this number is best put into perspective

TABLE 33

Patterns of Successive Maternal Utterances in which She Combines Corrective Feedback with other Teaching Techniques

Pattern	Observed freq., n_{ij}	Expected freq., e_{ij}[a]	z[b]	Pattern	Observed freq., n_{ij}	Expected freq., e_{ij}[a]	z[b]
40–24	25	20	1.4	81–28	36	8	13.9
81–40	23	3	16.3	81–81	24	2	24.3
40–29	22	18	1.2	81–40	23	3	16.3
40–25	20	17	1.2	81–24	18	12	2.4
40–40	20	5	9.4	81–25	16	10	2.7
28–40	20	14	2.3	81–51	15	6	5.1
40–27	19	17	0.6	81–2	13	8	2.4
80–40	17	10	2.8	1–81	12	4	5.4
2–40	15	14	0.5	29–81	11	11	0.1
40–28	13	14	−0.2	81–27	9	10	−0.4
40–80	12	10	0.7	2–81	7	8	−0.5
40–23	11	8	1.7	81–6	5	3	1.5
40–51	10	10	0.0	81–22	4	4	0.1

88

40–22	9	6	1.4	81–26	4	2	2.3
51–40	8	10	−0.8	27–81	4	10	−2.6
40–58	8	3	3.9	81–7	4	2	2.0
24–40	8	20	−3.6				
25–40	8	17	−2.8				
0–40	7	11	−1.5				
40–81	7	3	3.5				
40–0	7	11	−1.5				
40–26	7	4	1.9				
27–40	6	17	−3.5				
1–40	5	7	−0.9				
40–99	5	10	−2.1				
40–61	4	7	−1.6				
26–40	4	4	−0.1				
23–40	4	8	−1.7				

$^a e_{ij} = N_2 n_i n_j / N_1^2$

$^b z = \dfrac{n_{ij} - e_{ij}}{\sqrt{n_i p_j O}}$

by repeating the total number of pairs counted; it was 28,914. Of this, 300 is an almost infinitely small number, and it is also considerably smaller than those pairs containing obvious positive feedback in the form of code 80, $N = 689$. Around 15 obvious corrections per hour of interaction certainly should not be discounted, and could even have a profound effect, considering the overwhelmingly positive feedback the mother provides. They would probably stand out from this positive background and demand special attention from the child. Yet there is no question that Eve's mother is highly successful at maintaining a positive atmosphere and that she provides most of her corrections "on the sly." Therefore it is astonishing that the transcripts contain a remark that Eve went through a period of quite intensive stuttering. A special study will attempt to see whether any causes for these reported dysfluences can be detected in the transcripts.

Triple sequences of strategies and techniques. All the foundations have been laid in the previous sections to proceed now to the more complex and interesting topics pertaining to longer sequences of interactions which hopefully could provide some insights into mutual feedback patterns and the results of these feedbacks. Considerable problems are, however, encountered in this endeavor. The main one lies in the number of categories chosen for the analysis of strategies and techniques, namely 38 strategies of the child and 40 techniques of the mother, and the resulting number of possible triples, which is 78 to the third power or 474,552. With such a high number of possible triples, the sample of interactions would have to be extremely large for the triples to attain their random distributions. It could be seen from previous tables that the probability of occurrence for even the most frequent items was only around .05, and was lower for most of the items. If, for example, probabilities of .05, .04, and .03 are multiplied to estimate the joint probability of a triple sequence, this joint probability is .00006. To obtain an average expected frequency of at least 10 per triples, the total number of triples would have to be around 170,000. Since the total number of triples encountered in the ten samples analyzed in the present study is only 45,530, the expected frequencies of triples are on the average only around three, and even the frequencies for strong patterns cannot be expected to be very high. If even the strongest patterns obtain frequencies far below 100 in 20 hours of interactions and in a set containing over 45.000 triples, then the psychological impact of individual triple sequences has to be judged as almost nil. A different approach to longer sequences needs therefore to be chosen.

This approach will be based not upon individual techniques/strategies and their sequential dependencies, but on equivalence classes of techniques and the latters' sequential dependencies. Each of these equivalence classes can then be represented by any one of its members in the same manner as, in a sentence, each constituent slot can be filled by a large number of members from a specific word class. The establishment of such equivalence classes of strategies and techniques still requires considerable theoretical and practical work. The present approach will therefore have to be less ambitious. Since equivalence classes have not yet been established, the actual selections of various strategies and techniques after specific criterion behaviors will be sketched out in the following three figures. This will be done in a two-step sequence, as seen in the general design of all three figures. As a first element, a criterion behavior is chosen either of the child or the mother. This is the left-most item in the figures. Then, in the column headed "Second Element," those strategies of the child, in the upper part of the figures, and techniques of the mother, in the lower part of the figures, are given that followed the criterion behavior. Finally, in the right hand field of the figures, all the third elements of the triples are given—the strategies of the child always above the line that extends from each specific second element, and the techniques of the mother always below this line. Figure 5, for example, contains the following sequences: Child–Child–Child, Child–Child–Mother, Child–Mother–Child, and Child–Mother–Mother. The patterns are the same in Figure 6, and in Figure 7 the only difference is that all patterns begin with a technique of the mother. Three criterion behaviors were selected to explore the most important language phenomena: the child's vocabulary perseveration, code 29, in Figure 5; the child's spontaneous syntactic productions, code 51, in Figure 6; and the mother's instruction in minor morphemes, the functors as they often are called, code 2, in Figure 7. Only those triples are included in the three figures which appeared at least three times in the interactions, i.e., just minimally above the expected chance cooccurrences. By far, not all triples can therefore be interpreted as established interactional patterns.

In Figure 5, Eve's vocabulary perseveration is chosen as a uniform starting point. The second utterance in the triplet can then be one of the child or of the mother, and the same applies to the third step. The instances in which the second utterance is produced by the child will be considered first. They are found in the upper part of the figure, above the double line being drawn from the criterion code across the entire page. The most frequent strategy of Eve after a 29 is a second 29. The other techniques of the child in step 2 suggest that this two-step vocabulary perseveration is incorporated into and combined with syntactic exercises, i.e., build-ups, code 22, break-downs, code 23, constituent replacements, code 25, and several kinds of transformations or elaborations, codes 24, 27, 28, and 55. A very similar situation is encountered in step 3, when it is produced by the child and follows the child's turn in step 2. Vocabulary perseveration, code 29, is again dominant and it is almost exclusively accompanied by the diverse syntactic variations (codes in the 20s and code 51.) As suggested by the frequent codes 51 in step three, Eve seems to employ the redundancy between nonverbal and verbal structures in addition to the redundancies given by her self-repetitions, i.e., the 20-codes.

Continuing with the analysis of the Child–Child pattern, when it is now

Figure 5.   Triple sequences initiated by Eve's vocabulary perseveration.

followed in step three by a maternal response, it is to be noted that only five triples are encountered that follow this pattern. In three of these five patterns, i.e., 29–24–2, 29–29–2, and 29–29–24, the mother emphasizes bound or minor morphemes in addition to the vocabulary items stressed by Eve. The vocabulary item can be once more repeated by the mother, code 29, and optional transformations might be added, code 28. The distribution of maternal and child utterances in step three, as indicated by the top of Figure 5, is, however, misleading. The total numbers of Child–Child–Mother sequences are considerably higher than the Child–Child–Child sequences, only most Child–Child–Mother patterns appear less than three times and were therefore not included in Figure 5. In interactional terms, Eve is more prone to produce a triplet by repeating mostly the code 29 in step 3, probably often in combination with the code 51, whereas the mother is more versatile in how she reacts to two consecutive utterances of Eve.

Turning now to those sequences in which the second step of the triple is occupied by a maternal utterance, i.e., the lower part of Figure 5, it can be seen that the overall pattern is not too different from that seen just above. Code 1 for the mother corresponds to code 20 of the child; code 6, incorporation, for the mother's technique resembles closely code 22 for the child's strategy; and finally code 9 and 25 are partly equivalent for mother and child respectively. In interactional terms, exact repetition and repetition with elaboration or substitution are techniques that have been adopted by child and mother in the context of trying to incorporate a new or rare word into Eve's vocabulary. In addition, the mother also employs, in step 2 of the triple sequence, codes 23, 24, 27, 28, and most of all 29. It has to be remembered that the original 29 of the child represents a repetition, often of the mother's model. If the mother responds now to this with utterances coded in the twenty categories, this maternal self-repetition is fully comparable with the self-repetition of the child seen in step 2 in the upper half of Figure 5. The main difference between mother and child in step 2 lies therefore in the mother's use of more intentional instructional techniques, such as the codes 53, asking for a label, and code 80, reward.

And even in step 3, there are considerable similarities between the upper and lower part of Figure 5. The child is prone to employ vocabulary perseveration, and so is the mother, and so were both when the child produced the second element of the triple. And if the mother employed code 29 or code 80 in step 2, then she uses the techniques of syntactic variations, codes 23 to 28, in step 3. After the mother emphasized the vocabulary item in step 2, code 29, Eve employs syntactic variations on her previous utterance in step 3, or she imitates the mother and/or herself. Code 9 probably stands for triple sequences of the vocabulary item in question. A slight maternal tendency toward bound-morpheme teaching is noticed following her code 80, as seen in the codes 2 and 24.

After these detailed descriptions, a brief summary might sharpen the picture: Both mother and child show a strong tendency toward massed rehearsal in the case of vocabulary learning/teaching. This massed rehearsal is widely combined with syntactic variations. The latter would allow the child to recognize the selection restrictions and privileges of occurrence of the word in question. A large degree of redundancy is utilized by both. This redundancy derives mainly from the preceding utterances of one of the partners, but it can also consist of mapping between features of nonverbal reality and utterance structures. The two main differences between the interaction partners lie in the fact that the mother employs direct reward, code 80, and Eve relies repeatedly upon redundancy from situational structures, which the mother does not.

Figure 6 deals with syntactic endeavors of the child and the mother's utilization of such attempted mapping of reality structures upon linguistic ones. The somewhat brief discussion will follow the same pattern as that pertaining to Figure 5. A striking contrast to Figure 5 is encountered in the top half of Figure 6, that is, those patterns where Eve produces both the first and

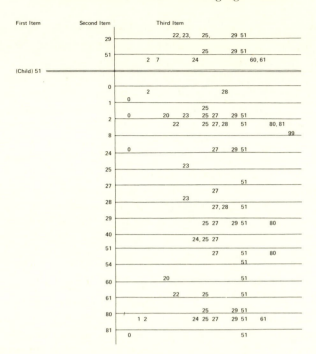

Figure 6.   Triple sequences initiated by Eve's syntactic mapping.

second utterance of the triple; only two quite simple strategies are encountered in step 2, i.e., codes 29 and 51. And even in step 3 this impression of restriction and rigidity is maintained. Mainly self-repetitions in similar form,
code 51, or in reduced form, codes 29 and 23, are encountered on Eve's part,
the only exceptions being codes 22 and 25, appearing three times. It almost
appears as if Eve, after the exertion of encoding reality in a syntactic structure,
ran out of steam and just managed to repeat her achievement in full or in part.
The mother's responses in step 3 of the sequence provide a similar suggestion
of incompleteness and insufficiency in the child's performance. Codes 60 and
61 represent leading and guiding questions; codes 2 and 7 are two forms of expansion, one pertaining mainly to minor morphemes and the other to more
important constituents; and code 24 indicates also an addition of semantically
minor bound morphemes.

In contrast to this overall impression of restriction in Eve's consecutive
second and third utterances, the interactions become richer and more
versatile when the mother takes over in step 2, after the child tried to map reality upon language. The mother imitates and expands, codes 1, 2, and 8; she
helps the child to improve in her performance through the guiding questions
of code 60 and 61, or to elaborate upon it through the question coded 54. She
praises quite often, code 80, but does not shy away from corrections, codes 40
and 81. She might model the mapping, code 51, and in her self-repetitions

she employs the more complex forms, codes 24, 25, 27, 28, that is, transformations, replacements, or morpheme perseverations. This intervening maternal booster seems to be quite helpful for Eve. In step 3, quite some of Eve's utterances entail the more complex strategies of 25 and 27, although the codes suggesting mainly repetition, i.e., codes 20, 29, and 51, still predominate. The mother retains in step 3 her approach of step 2, and follows up predominantly with complex codes of 24, 25, 27, and 28. Since the topic is mostly retained by the mother, the simpler codes of vocabulary perseveration and repeated mapping, 29 and 51, accompany her more complex ones as an almost necessary consequence of semantic continuity and multiple coding. Some reward, code 80, is added in step 3 if it wasn't done in step 2.

In summary: Eve seems to experience considerable problems in mapping reality structures into language without the immediate help from her mother. This conclusion is supported by even a superficial reading of the transcripts, and it was to be expected, considering Eve's age. Eve's performance is generally restricted and limited in alternatives. Mostly her mother rises, however, immediately to the occasion, and joins the endeavor in step 2 of the three-step sequence. This intervention leads to more advanced performance by Eve in step 3, and the mother herself can make her "language lesson" more complex if she retains the floor in Step 3.

Finally, in Figure 7, it shall be explored what happens when the mother attempts to add minor functors, the later appearing and seemingly more difficult elements of language, to an utterance of Eve. The first step is therefore occupied by a maternal utterance, code 2, the type of expansion that was originally described by R. Brown. It is quite evident in the top half of Figure 7 that Eve does not handle this type of input very well. She responds either with an uncodable utterance, code 0, a reduced imitation, code 2, vocabulary items, codes 29 and 50, or a reduced self-repetition, code 23. Whereas codes 22, 25, and 51 suggest a more advanced response, her mother employs her technique of expansion, code 2, after all these three strategies, or she obviously corrects Eve, code 40. Both types of maternal response strongly suggest that even these responses of Eve still missed the items the mother wanted to convey. Even more impressive as to Eve's processing difficulties, no single triple of the type Mother–Child–Child attained a frequency of at least three instances so that it could have been included in Figure 7. The maternal code 80 that follows in step 3 in four triples might easily represent an attempt at camouflage or encouragement. It is provided in half of the triples for vocabulary items which were not the main topic to be taught. To show this and to explore the function of the maternal technique 25, the actual utterance sequences need to be explored. In summary, it appears that Eve, if left to her own devices, does only minimally profit from the mother's provision of minor functors—at least during the age period studied. The mother's contribution in step 3 shows that she doesn't give up easily, even if Eve is not yet ready for a specific skill. Her preponderant technique is coded 2, i.e., insistence upon

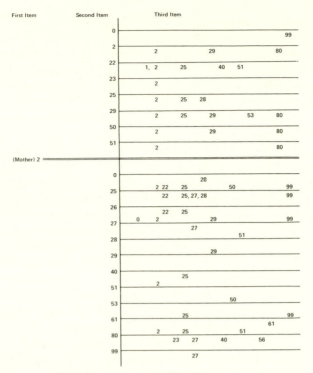

Figure 7. Triple sequences initiated by maternal expansions.

the minor functors she began to provide, followed by code 25, replacement sequences in her own utterance in order to clarify the syntactic structure. A reasonable number of rewards, code 80, is provided to reassure the child.

As shown in the lower section of Figure 7, the mother employs more complex techniques when she follows up on her original intent in step 2. The more complex codes involving transformations, codes 27 and 28, teaching questions, 53 and 61, and replacement sequences, codes 25 and 26, predominate. Reward, code 80, is dispensed liberally too. It befits the occasion when the mother tried to introduce minor functors that the quite rare code 26, replacement sequence of minor elements, appears. Eve's strategies in step 3, after a maternal second element, suggest that she still might be close to being overtaxed in her capacity. Her strategies in step 3 are almost identical to those she produced in step 2, i.e., mainly simple ones, codes 0, 2, and 50. There are, however, three triples with the strategy 25 and two with the strategy 51 that appear more complex and need exploring. Most of the other strategies suggest that the maternal elaboration did not bear fruit. The mother continues in step 3 with the more complex categories, again involving many transformations, some corrections, and a rare dynamic elaboration, code 56. Since the mother has had the floor for three steps in a row, any reward could only apply to herself, would therefore be quite meaningless, and does not appear in the lower part of Figure 7.

In summary: Expansion with minor functors is certainly provided by the mother—the total frequency of this maternal technique is 623—but Eve is not yet ready for this type of complex linguistic instruction. The effect even after maternal elaboration seems to be quite weak. When casting a summarizing glance back at all three figures discussed in this last section, the results are quite illuminating. In the case of vocabulary learning, code 29, the triple sequences suggested that Eve was quite successful in attaining the goals. In the case of major syntactic mapping, code 51, Eve seemed to seriously stumble without maternal help, but she showed more advanced language patterns in step 3 after maternal intervention. In the case of minor morpheme elaboration, code 2, which is known to be mastered latest in language acquisition, it does not seem to matter much whether the mother elaborates and repeats her model, also in step 2; Eve's output in step 3 and step 2 is almost undistinguishable and weak. These patterns, as they seem to appear from the figures, are in such good agreement with the commonly established knowledge of child language acquisition that they can serve to support the construct validity of the present categorizations and analyses. It has, however, to be admitted that many of the suggested interpretations still need qualitative checking on the basis of the actual syntactic and morphological items that are or are not acquired. This checking has only partly been done, and the results will fill a separate report.

Selected examples as they were presented are very helpful in elucidating meaningful instructional and learning patterns. Being selected, they also entail, however, the danger of providing a skewed and possibly even distorted picture. To counteract this, two types of triple sequences will be presented in Table 34—the last table of this report, to assure the reader—chosen only in respect to the frequencies of their appearance. Those two types were chosen that encompassed specific triples that were relatively frequent as compared to the expected frequencies, which were in the range of 3 to at most 5 instances per pattern. The two types fitting this criterion were Child–Mother–Mother and Mother–Mother–Mother triples. The first ten patterns of each of these two types are presented in Table 34.

Even a preliminary perusal of Table 34 shows that the patterns under the two types differ considerably. Eight of the ten most frequent patterns initiated by Eve deal with the relatively elementary tasks of vocabulary acquisition and the mapping of reality structures upon linguistic ones. In respect to the theoretically interesting question of reinforcement for the child's attempts at language acquisition, it is impressive to see that eight of these ten most frequent triples contain a maternal token of reward, code 80. As argued above, maternal techniques, coded 2, can fulfill a similar reward function. Besides providing this reward, the mother mainly repeats either the vocabulary item, code 29, or the syntactic mapping, code 51. She may also expand Eve's

TABLE 34
A Few Selected Preliminary Examples of Intensive Maternal
Intervention in Triple Sequences

Pattern C – M – M	Observed[a] frequency	Exp. F e_{ijk}[b]	Pattern M – M – M	Observed[a] frequency	Exp. F e_{ijk}[b]
29 – 80 – 29	28	2.8	25 – 25 – 25	24	4.5
29 – 29 – 80	25	2.8	29 – 29 – 29	16	5.8
51 – 80 – 2	22	1.5	28 – 25 – 25	14	3.6
51 – 80 – 51	17	1.1	2 – 25 – 25	11	3.7
2 – 80 – 2	15	1.1	28 – 28 – 28	10	2.3
29 – 29 – 29	14	4.9	28 – 28 – 25	10	2.9
51 – 51 – 80	12	1.1	28 – 28 – 24	9	3.5
51 – 2 – 80	11	1.5	28 – 24 – 24	9	5.2
51 – 2 – 27	11	2.5	25 – 25 – 28	8	3.6
25 – 80 – 2	10	1.5	28 – 25 – 28	8	2.9

[a]These are total frequencies from all ten samples.
[b]$e_{ijk} = p_i \cdot p_j \cdot p_k \cdot N_3$
N_3 = Total number of triplets

utterance with minor functors, code 2, and only in one of the patterns does she employ any obvious transformations, code 27. In four of the five instances when Eve tried to map environmental structures into syntactic ones, code 51, the mother provides a reward, code 80, and in all five instances she repeats and expands the child's syntactic structures, codes 2 and 51. The other two possibly complex strategies of Eve, codes 2 and 25, are both followed by maternal reward and expanding imitation. The general impression derived from the left side of Table 34 is one of simplicity, redundancy, and rehearsal. The right hand side, with a sequence of three successive maternal utterances, presents a quite contrasting impression. The predominant code is 28, optional transformations, which is closely followed by code 25, replacements of major sentence constituents. Three triples contain the codes 2 or 24, i.e., they deal with minor functors. Much opportunity for syntax learning is provided in almost all of these triples. Only the one triple consisting of thrice the code 29 deals with the simple task of vocabulary acquisition.

Considering these triple sequences of the mother, the question of why the mother produced them arises immediately. Knowledge of transcripts and the frequent techniques coded 25 and 28 suggest that at least some of the patterns are repair sequences. The first pattern, three times the technique 25, is one of the most typical repair sequences: The mother repeatedly replaces vocabulary items in one or several sentence constituents in order to increase the chance that Eve might analyze the sentence. Both the easier, i.e., more common, vocabulary items substituted and the greater obviousness of the syntactic structure, attained through the process of replacing elements, increase this chance for Eve. In addition, the mother often adds questions, code 28, in order to guide Eve in the desired direction. With these suggestions of repair sequences, the need for the analysis of longer sequence of interactions becomes most obvious. Not only would it be of great interest to see where Eve failed, but it might be even more important to find out when, if, and whether the mother succeeded with her repairs or not.

At this point, when the discussion has arrived at the most interesting topics, it shall be, at least temporarily, interrupted. Not only does the statistical methodology still need to be worked out for the parsimonious establishment of these longer sequences; to really make these complex analyses meaningful, qualitative analyses of the actual sentences produced and improved upon have to be added. Challenging topics remain therefore for future reports.

DISCUSSION

Since the endeavor to analyze mother-child interactions exhaustively is quite complex, and since even the present partial analysis was quite lengthy, the first concern regards what has been achieved or at least attempted, and what some of the remaining tasks are. The latter can be surveyed more briefly and shall be discussed first.

The Open Tasks

The next step to be undertaken is the analysis of multiple instructional and learning techniques/strategies. After sequential cooccurrences have been explored in the major sections of this study, simultaneous cooccurrences are needed to complete the description of maternal teaching and the child's learning. Such cooccurrences could also supply partial answers to the most interesting questions about what is taught/learned by these techniques/ strategies. If, for example, the codes for imitation are mostly combined with the code 29, Vocabulary Perseveration, one of the uses of imitation would be indicated. If, in contrast, imitation codes are mostly combined with the codes 24, Morpheme Perseveration, or 51, Syntactic Mapping, it could be concluded that imitation is mainly employed for morphological and syntactic learning.

Admittedly the best approach to answer these questions and the next open task is the integration of the analyses of techniques and strategies presented in this study with the data on the content of the instructions. Although a few items pertaining to the content of instructions have been presented, the difficult task of integrating these two data sets has not yet been begun. Only if it is known whether and which specific methodologies are optimally suited for the conveying of specific linguistic skills can the observational findings be employed in intervention techniques aimed at specific linguistic delays or handicaps.

Both theoretically and practically important is another aspect concerning the relationships between techniques and contents of instruction. It has been repeatedly mentioned in the study that specific contents seemed to be presented by the mother and acted upon by the child in rhythmic patterns. After their introduction and massed rehearsal, repetitions with increasingly longer intervals seemed to follow. This was observed mainly in respect to vocabulary training/learning, but indications exist that it may be even more pronounced when new syntactic structures are introduced. If this could be demonstrated quantitatively, it would not only contribute heavily to a learning-theoretical interpretation of language acquisition, it would also have profound implications for the practical tasks of remedial language teaching.

Since practical implications were mentioned repeatedly and are certainly envisaged as long-run outcomes of these studies, another important question has to be faced, that of the generalizability of the results from the present dyad to other ones coming from different socio-economic classes and composed in part or totally of male members. Considerable evidence has been accumulated regarding differences between paternal and maternal instructional styles, and idiosyncratic differences between children have been generally reported. In the present study too, the coding of the interactions of Adam with his mother indicated that partially different phenomena are to be expected. Social class differences in verbal interactions have been demonstrated consistently during the last decades. Since a sample of one dyad can give no assurance about generalizability, and since universality of the principles cannot be assumed, differential evidence about generalizability or the lack of it has to be accumulated before meaningful applications can be attempted.

It is obvious that, even with optimal planning, by far not all questions can be conceptualized that might arise in the course of years of research on first language acquisition. It is therefore intended to code the transcripts as exhaustively as possible for computer storage of the data and to develop a format for flexible access to these data. Once the data are stored on computers, they can be easily employed for the evaluation of new and of very specific questions that arise.

The Achievements

It appears that what has been done or at least attempted can be summarized under five major headings. This retrospective assessment will follow the sequential design of the study but it will be structured differently.

(a) It was—the first time it appears—attempted to systematically and encompassingly differentiate levels of analysis in the study of child–mother interactions. Four major levels were differentiated: the content level as expressed in topics and their boundaries, the illocutionary force, the linguistic skills that were taught and learned, and the instructional and learning methods. The first, the content, was only touched upon in a global manner, for two reasons: First, semantics is only of relatively minor interest for the goals of the present study. Second, research on the structure and organization of the semantic field is by far not yet advanced enough to make it possible to include an established category system into a project that has a different focus. Complex and specific research endeavors would be required to advance in this area.

The distinctions made for millenia by grammarians and in lay terminology, and the recent philosophical analyses of everyday language, made it possible to employ a quite well established system for the description of the Illocutionary Force of the interactions. Although this area is not of any major concern for the present study, it was considered advisable to include this level, since diverse and interesting relationships across levels are expected to exist. Some of them have been indicated, as, e.g., the fact that the mother's questions that arise from illocutionary exigencies, incidentally provide an optimal training for transformations. Though this category system is well established, improvements certainly can be made. For example, code 1, Declarative Sentence/Utterance, is so broad and so frequent in the transcripts that meaningful subdivisions could be made. Also, illocutionary processes in instructional settings, such as in classrooms, have to be studied to see whether the presently employed set sufficiently covers the illocutionary phenomena arising in the specific situation of instruction.

The scope pertaining to instructional content is so wide that selections of items to study had of necessity to be made. The method employed at present to make these selections was less than ideal, since the latter were not made in accordance with one consistent criterion. Minor bound and free morphemes were studied mainly because of historical reasons, i.e., because R. Brown has analyzed their developmental history in Eve and has drawn strong, often quoted, and in the opinion of the writer highly questionable conclusions. In contrast, the choice of the main syntactic frames for analysis was based upon not-yet-well-established psychological and linguistic hypotheses regarding a differentiation of two basic and widely found frames and the transformations applied to them. Finally, reasons to include specific sentence constituents stem from age-old grammatical systems of syntactic analysis. For the full explanation of language acquisition, more systematic approaches might be chosen. Or, more probably, unsystematic findings will be integrated after decades of studies that centered almost randomly upon a few aspects of the linguistic code.

The main level of the present analysis was that of instructional techniques and learning strategies. Although the system of analysis could incorporate R. Brown's (Brown & Bellugi, 1964) path-breaking observations and could build upon the conceptualizations contributed by many authors, and especially by Cross (1977), it was conceived in a somewhat different and more differentiated manner. In spite of the relatively large number of categories employed, it is almost certain that the present system is not exhaustive. Not only were phonetic aspects omitted, but especially the teaching of the large variety of transformations was only touched upon in a few categories: codes 27 and 28 for simple sentences, and codes 58 and 59 for complex ones. Much finer differentiations will be needed to explain how children acquire the complex rules described by linguists under the term "transformations." In retrospect, it is also obvious that a clean separation of the level of instructional contents and the level of instructional methods has not yet been attained in all categories. Since the present approach represents only a systematic beginning, much room for improvement is found in most aspects.

(b) The second major endeavor of the present study lies in the systematic application of interactional approaches. This was done by means of presenting cooccurrences of doubles and triples and by comparing them with their expected probabilities. Where needed, transitional probabilities were added. Besides these single, joint, and transitional probabilities and the pertinent frequencies that were actually presented, the possibilities inherent in lagged probabilities and higher order Markov models have been briefly alluded to. One of the main difficulties arising from the simultaneous need for longer sequences of interactions and for a large number of instructional categories was spelled out. A first attempt to solve this dilemma was made in the form of a preliminary search for equivalence classes. But clear criteria for the establishment of such equivalent classes still have to be worked out. More generally, the solution will lie in model testing approaches in contrast to merely descriptive or null hypothesis testing ones. Whereas statistical methods for such model testing approaches for quantitative data have been developed in engineering for spectral analysis (e.g. Jenkins & Watts, 1969), no equivalent techniques have yet been found by the writer for qualitative/categorical data. Since quite distinct hypotheses can be formulated (e.g., Moerk, 1976), it should, however, not be difficult to at least evaluate how closely they accord with the data.

(c) With this emphasis upon transitional probabilities and mother–child interactions, the focus has been profoundly shifted in the approach to cause-effect analyses of language acquisition. Most previous studies (e.g. Brown, 1973; Nelson, 1973) relied upon the measurement of effects a considerable time after the causes had been ascertained and thereby upon cross lagged covariations. The present approach aims at causes in the microanalytic sense of quite immediate cause-effect relations. This contrast was carefully elaborated by K. Lewin (1951) under the terminology of "historical versus systematic causation." In these terms: The present study was aimed at finding in the immediately preceding maternal input the systematic causes for the child's language performance, which often involved improvements as compared to preceding utterances, i.e., linguistic progress. Certainly, problems remain on the theoretical and factual level. As Bandura (e.g., 1973) has repeatedly spelled out, the acquisition of a new skill does not need immediately to lead to its performance, so that an absence of immediate effects cannot automatically lead to a refutation of the effectiveness of the input. If, however, as is often the case in verbal interactions, the child attempts to produce linguistic utterances that are closely related to the input, an absence of traces of the input can be more assuredly interpreted as an absence of effects. To be certain, lagged behaviors over shorter and longer intervals have to be investigated. If, even after gradually increasing intervals, no effect of specific instances of input can be discovered in the utterances of the child, then such effects can probably be discounted due to the large amount of information input and limitations in short- and intermediate-term memory span. Implied in this preceding sentence is, however, the assumption that more processing time and/or considerable activity is required on the side of the child before items can be transferred from a short- and intermediate-term to long-term memory. This assumption still needs evaluation. More theoretically, it is postulated that only the study of systematic causality can lead to an understanding of the cause-effect processes. What was measured commonly as cause-effect relations over longer intervals confounds immediate cause-effect sequences that are retained in a pure form, those that were altered in the intervals, intervening causes which were not measured but produced the effects measured, and the elimination of originally obtained effects due to intervening influences or just to forgetting.

The interest in the causes of language acquisition led naturally to previously suggested causal hypotheses, most of all to Brown's (1973) conclusions about the lack of causal effects. Following Bandura's (1977) differentiation and terminology, antecedent determinants and consequent determinants will be discussed separately.

(d) In the context of language learning, the hypothesized antecedent determinants are the maternal models. Two possible effects of maternal models have been the focus of lively controversy in the recent past. The *immediate* effect, which was argued about mostly under the motto whether imitation is progressive, and the effect of input *frequency*, which was vigorously denied by Brown (1973). In the present report, no systematic study of the effects of imitation has been made yet, though several indications for its effectiveness were mentioned and references were cited that supported such effects. Brown (1973) had, however, provided detailed evidence as to Eve's progress in certain linguistic items, that is, minor functors. These developments could be related to input frequencies and another mostly neglected factor, namely the acoustic distinctiveness of the items. For the specific morphemes studied, acoustic distinctiveness and input frequency appeared to be the major determining factors in Eve's linguistic progress. It was therefore suggested that, for the early stages, a focus upon the more simple processes of perception and storage might be more fruitful than that upon the perhaps overemphasized cognitive aspects. Since the value of the input frequencies had been reaffirmed, preliminary data concerning the overwhelming amounts of input were provided. Since the input is so abundant, and since the child progresses relatively gradually in her mastery, as was strongly emphasized by Brown (1973), any hypothesis testing explanation applied to most aspects of early language acquisition is in serious theoretical trouble.

(e) As consequent determiners, rewards and corrections provided as maternal feedback have been focused upon. Since Brown and associates (Brown, 1973; Brown, Cazden, & Bellugi, 1969; Brown & Hanlon, 1970) have published their decided opinions about the absence of any trace of these forms of feedback for linguistic progress or failure, authors dealing with these topics have largely and often unquestioningly accepted and repeated these opinions. Since little integrated and closely pertinent evidence existed, they often had little choice to do otherwise. Yet the related information that did exist from comparable situations was mostly neglected. For example, Streissguth and Bee (1972) reported a study in which college-educated mothers verbally taught a nonverbal task to their infants. They found a high number of verbal positive reinforcements (e.g., "Good girl") that exceeded the negative feedback in a proportion of 4 to 1. Hess and Shipman (1967) reported similar tactics of praise that were employed by their middle-class mothers. Feshbach (1973) commented upon the predominance of positive reinforcement in middle class dyads, when the task was the teaching/learning of reading. For verbal interactions and language learning, Moerk (1976, 1978) provided detailed examples and frequencies for these various types of rewarding and motivating feedback. There exist, of course, many studies in the behavioristic tradition that have very similar implications, even if the methods were mostly not naturalistic and observational.

Due to this contrast between the prevailing opinion and the available data, it was considered worthwhile to reevaluate this question on the basis of parts of the data Brown and associates employed themselves. As has been seen in the last part of the Result section, this reevaluation resulted in findings diametrically opposed to those obtained by Brown and associates. Since the contrasting conclusions were reached on the basis of partly identical transcripts, a clarification of this contrast is called for. It cannot be fully provided, since the criteria Brown and associates employed to rule out these types of feedback are not fully known to the writer. But there is no question that Brown observed a large number of "corrections" in the technique "imitation through expansion" discovered by him. It is also quite evident from the transcripts that Brown found ample instances wherein the mother repeated or reformulated utterances of the child in an improved form without expanding it—which is a form of correction too. It seems therefore as if Brown's term "corrections" really refers only to "negative corrections," i.e., corrections that have a strong negative emotional component, e.g., "You are wrong . . . ." If Brown defined his "corrections" in such a manner, then his data and conclusions are in close accordance: The mother almost never chastises Eve in the course of language instruction. But it is suggested that a correction does not need to be a reprimand. Corrections can be provided in a constructive and mainly informative manner. They can also be emotionally neutralized by tokens of reward, as shown in the Result section.

Similarly to "corrections" it is suggested that terminological problems led to misunderstandings in the case of "reward" too. It is agreed that mothers do not have at hand a Skinner box from which pops out a reward after every response—which might be the underlying paradigm that was argued against. But Eve's mother is something like a computerized Skinner box, dispensing every two to three minutes on the average a token of reward, mostly in the form of "Yes." That these rewards are dispensed not randomly, but in meaningful relationships to the preceding linguistic strategies of the child, has been demonstrated in the tables and figures of the Result section. A controversy could, however, arise whether it is acceptable to code a maternal "Yes" in the same category as a maternal "Good" or some other more obviously positive feedback and to interpret it as reward. To defend this decision, it would be an easy task to enumerate many studies done with a behavioristic/operant conditioning/behavior modification background that have shown how effective the "Yes" of a therapist or any reward dispenser can be. These findings are well enough known and don't need to be documented. The decision to interpret a "Yes" as a reward was, however, mainly based upon more closely pertinent experiences and reasons. In the past as a student, and now as a teacher, the principal investigator has observed almost innumerable times the differential effects a "Yes" and a "No" can produce in the emotional or overt response of the receiver of this feedback if the dispenser of the feedback is in the position of teacher or, more generally, of authority. This naturalistic situation might be less well documented in psychological publications, but it is certainly not less well known and not less real. If "Yes" and "No" are accepted as reward and punishment, respectively, when dispensed by the mother in language performance situations, then the evidence in Brown's data is convincing that this reward and punishment is dispensed for overall acceptibility/inacceptibility of the message and only occasionally for its truth value. Although acceptibility means linguistic wellformedness to a certain degree, it does not imply grammatical perfection.

With the last two points discussed, a mostly well hidden error source was touched upon: Concepts can be operationally defined for an investigation so that the intension and the extension of the concept do not coincide with the intensions and extensions employed when the identical label is used in lay terminology or in the scientific field in question. Two or more different entities are therefore referred to, but the identical label hides these differences and produces the impression of a uniform concept. Every reader of the investigation in question might therefore conceptualize a different entity and might draw different conclusions due to his specific conceptualizations. Terminological precautions have to be exercised also in regard to the present study. The reader was forewarned on the first page of the introduction that the theoretical orientation leans towards a teaching/learning interpretation. The techniques/strategies were consequently conceptualized on the basis of this orientation. If this conceptualization could be proven as an incorrect preconceptualization, much of the interpretation propounded in this study would have to be reevaluated and possibly reformulated. Since it is strongly believed that the approach is basically correct, the following conclusions are proposed: The maternal input is rich enough, provided frequently enough, based upon enough semantic and linguistic redundancy, and is provided with a degree of instructional sophistication as far as its contingency relationships are concerned, that it suffices to explain even the accelerated language development of Eve—given an intelligent child with a good cognitive basis upon which to conceive meanings for communication. With sufficient attention given to careful microanalyses, the exact teaching/learning methods mother and child employ, and their results, can be demonstrated.

References

Bakeman, R. Untangling streams of behavior: Sequential analyses of observation data. In G. P. Sackett (Ed.), *Observing behavior* (Vol. II). *Data collection and analysis methods*. Baltimore, Md: University Park Press, 1978.

Bandura, A. *Aggression: A social learning analysis*. Englewood Cliffs, NJ: Prentice-Hall, 1973.

Bandura, A. *Social learning theory*. Englewood Cliffs, NJ: Prentice-Hall, 1977.

Barker, R. G., & Wright, H. F. *Midwest and its children*. New York: Harper & Row, 1955.

Bloom, L., Hood, L., & Lightbown, P. Imitation in language development: If, when, and why. *Cognitive Psychology*, 1974, *6*, 380–420.

Brown, R. *A first language. The early stages*. Cambridge, MA: Harvard University Press, 1973.

Brown, R., & Bellugi, U. Three processes in the child's acquisition of syntax. *Harvard Educational Review*, 1964, *34*, 133–151.

Brown, R., Cazden, C., & Bellugi, U. The child's grammar from I to III. In J. P. Hill (Ed.), *Minnesota symposium on child psychology* (Vol. 2). Minneapolis, MN: University of Minnesota Press, 1969.

Brown, R., & Hanlon, C. Derivational complexity and order of acquisition in child speech. In J. R. Hayes (Ed.), *Cognition and the development of language*. New York: Wiley, 1970.

Buhler, K. *Sprachtheorie*. Jena: G. Fischer, 1934.

Chomsky, N. Skinner: Verbal behavior. *Language*, 1959, *35*, 26–57.

Clark, R. Performing without competence. *Journal of Child Language*, 1974, *1*, 1–10.

Clark, R. What's the use of imitation? *Journal of Child Language*, 1977, *4*, 341–358.

Cohen, J., & Cohen, P. *Applied multiple regression/correlation analysis for the behavioral sciences*. Hillsdale, NJ: Lawrence Erlbaum Assoc., 1975.

Collis, G. M., & Schaffer, H. R. Synchronization of visual attention in mother-infant pairs. *Journal of Child Psychology and Psychiatry*, 1975, *16*, 315–320.

Cross, T. Some relationships between motherese and linguistic level in accelerated children. *Papers and Reports on Child Language Development*, 1975, *10*, 117–135.

Cross, T. G. Mothers' speech adjustments: The contributions of selected child listener variables. In C. Ferguson & C. Snow (Eds.), *Talking to children: Language input and acquisition*. Cambridge: Cambridge University Press, 1977.

Drach, K. M. The language of the parent: A pilot study. In K. M. Drach, B. Kobashigawa, C. Pfuderer, & D. Slobin (Eds.), *The structure of linguistic input to children* (Language-Behavior Research Laboratory, Working Paper 14). Unpublished manuscript, University of California, Berkeley, January, 1969.

Feshbach, N. D. *Teaching styles of Israeli four-year-olds and their mothers*. Paper presented at the meeting of the American Educational Research Association. New Orleans, February 1973.

Forner, M. *The mother as LAD: Interaction between order and frequency of parental input and child production*. Paper presented at the meeting of the 6th Annual University of Minnesota Linguistics Symposium, March 1977.

Fraser, C., Bellugi, U., & Brown, R. Control of grammar in imitation, comprehension, and production. *Journal of Verbal Learning and Verbal Behavior*, 1963, 2, 121–135.

Gottman, J. M., & Bakeman, R. The sequential analysis of observational data. In M. E. Lamb, S. J. Suomi, & G. R. Stephenson (Eds.), *Social interaction analysis. Methodological issues*. Madison, WI: University of Wisconsin Press, 1979.

Gottman, J., Markman, H., & Notarius, C. The topography of marital conflict: A sequential analysis of verbal and nonverbal behavior. *Journal of Marriage and Family*, 1977, 39, 461–477.

Hess, R. D., & Shipman, V. C. Cognitive elements in maternal behavior. In J. P. Hill (Ed.), *Minnesota symposia on child psychology* (Vol. I). Minneapolis, MN: University of Minnesota Press, 1967.

Hunt, J. Intrinsic motivation and its role in psychological development. In D. Levine (Ed.), *Nebraska symposium on motivation*. Lincoln, NE: University of Nebraska Press, 1965.

Jenkins, G. M., & Watts, D. C. *Spectral analysis and its applications*. San Francisco, CA: Holden-Day, 1969.

Lewin, K. *Field theory in social science*. New York: Harper & Row, 1951.

MacWhinney, B. The acquisition of morphophonology. *Monographs of the Society for Research in Child Development*, 1978, 43, (1–2, Serial No. 174).

Maratsos, M. P., & Chalkley, M. A. The internal language of children's syntax: The ontogenesis and representation of syntactic categories. In K. Nelson (Ed.), *Children's language* (Vol. II). New York: Gardner Press, 1979.

Moerk, E. L. Principles of dyadic interaction in language learning. *Merrill-Palmer Quarterly*, 1972, 18, 229–257.

Moerk, E. L. Changes in verbal child-mother interactions with increasing language skills of the child. *Journal of Psycholinguistic Research*, 1974, 3, 101–116.

Moerk, E. L. Verbal interactions between children and their mothers during the preschool years. *Developmental Psychology*, 1975, 11, 788–794.

Moerk, E. L. Processes of language teaching and training in the interactions of mother-child dyads. *Child Development*, 1976, 47, 1064–1078. (a)

Moerk, E. L. Motivational variables in language acquisition. *Child Study Journal*, 1976, 6, 55–84. (b)

Moerk, E. L. Processes and products of imitation: Additional evidence that imitation is progressive. *Journal of Psycholinguistic Research*, 1977, 6, 187–202. (a)

Moerk, E. L. *Pragmatic and semantic aspects of early language development*. Baltimore, MD: University Park Press, 1977. (b)

Moerk, E. L. Determiners and consequences of verbal behaviors of young children and their mothers. *Developmental Psychology*, 1978, 14, 537–545.

Moerk, E. L. *Continuity in functions and structures that lead from preverbal achievements to the emergent phenomenon of language competence*. Paper presented at the meeting of the Conference of the International Society for Research in Behavioral Development, Lund, Sweden, June 1979.

Moerk, E. L. Relationships between parental input frequencies and children's language acquisition: A reanalysis of Brown's data. *Journal of Child Language*, 1980, 7, 105–118.

Moerk, E. L., & Moerk, C. Quotations, imitations, and generalizations. Factual and methodological analyses. *International Journal of Behavioral Development*, 1979, 2, 43–72.

Nelson, K. Structure and strategy in learning to talk. *Monographs of the Society for Research in Child Development*, 1973, 38, (1, 2, Serial No. 149).

Sackett, G. The lag sequential analysis of contingency and cyclicity in behavioral interaction research. In J. D. Osofsky (Ed.), *Handbook of infant development*. New York: John Wiley & Sons, 1979.

Savic, S. Aspects of adult-child communication: The problem of question acquisition. *Journal of Child Language*, 1975, 2, 251–260.

Searle, J. What is a speech act? In M. Black (Ed.), *Philosophy in America*. Cornell: Allen & Unwin, 1965.

Searle, J. R. *Speech acts*. London: Cambridge University Press, 1969.

Shatz, M. On the development of communicative understandings: An early strategy for interpreting and responding to messages. In J. Glick & A. Clarke-Stewart (Eds.), *Studies in social and cognitive development*. New York: Gardner Press, 1977.

Skinner, B. F. *Verbal behavior*. New York: Appleton-Century-Crofts, 1957.

Snow, E. Mother's speech to children learning language. *Child Development*, 1972, *43*, 549–565.

Streissguth, A. P., & Bee, H. L. Mother-child interactions and cognitive development in children. *Young Children*, 1972, 154–173.

Whitehurst, G. J. Imitation, response novelty, and language acquisition. In B. C. Etzel, J. M. LeBlanc, & D. M. Baer (Eds.), *New developments in behavioral research: Theory, method, and application. In honor of Sidney W. Bijou*. Hillsdale, NJ: Lawrence Erlbaum Assoc., 1977.

Zipff, G. K. *Human behavior and the principle of least effort*. Cambridge, MA: Addison-Wesley Press, 1949.

Appendices

The appendices are intended to provide an overall impression of the types of interactions between Eve and her mother and of the general emphases of the analyses. Since they contain the text, the code numbers, and the labels for the instructional methods, it is hoped that the character of the analyses that were discussed throughout much of the book becomes more obvious. Since few analyses of this encompassing type are found in the literature, the examples will enable the reader to obtain a better basis to evaluate this endeavor. The instructional methods are mainly provided for the utterances of the mother. Towards the end of the observation period, that is, with the higher utterance numbers, when Eve became more verbally involved, learning strategies of the child are exemplified too.

Under the column Instructional Contents, only some of the major aspects of language skills that appear to be exercised during the interactions are mentioned. In principle, each word of the conversation partners could constitute a language learning/rehearsal opportunity. Whereas this is certainly the case, rehearsals in areas which the child has mastered very well are of comparatively little importance for her language skills and of little interest in regard to the acquisition of linguistic skills. Linguistic items that Eve is just beginning to learn, and those that her mother obviously intends for her to analyze, since she wants to convey through them a specific message to her child, are for the present goals of greatest interest. These items are generally specified under Instructional Contents, although it is not asserted that they are captured exhaustively. The emphasis lies more upon exemplifying instructional aspects, such as repetitiveness, systematic alteration of retained themes, the sensitive responsiveness of the mother, etc., than upon systematic exhaustiveness.

The diverse appendices are introduced with a specific heading and some remarks that are intended to indicate the overall flavor of the interactional sequence presented. It is readily admitted that the same excerpts could be analyzed from quite different perspectives and could therefore appear under different headings. Again the headings serve the function of indicating for the reader some features that were deemed of importance and to help him to more meaningfully browse through these appendices. Finally, as Appendix 7, the interactions between Eve and her mother are provided for an entire hour, the first hour recorded by R. Brown and associates, together with the analyses suggested. This appendix is intended to demonstrate and emphasize the intensity of the instructional opportunities encountered even within a single hour of interaction. Again the analysis is not exhaustive, and a good deal more of instructional value could be demonstrated if the phonetic/phonemic aspects of the interactions were studied. But since the latter have been omitted also in the main text of the monograph, such analyses would not be directly relevant to the major goals of the study. It goes without saying that all the appendices, especially the last one, are also intended to enable the reader to critically evaluate the categorizations of instructional methods employed, and to see their use in actual application. This should make it easier to evaluate the overall endeavor provided in the monograph on the basis of at least some raw data.

Appendix 1 (Utterances 577 ff)

Appendix 1 was selected for two main reasons: First, it accords well with the emphasis upon pragmatics so often encountered in the recent literature. In this episode, the mother very obviously wants "to do something with words," namely to get her child to drink from a cup instead of spooning the fluid out of it. Since the mother does not formulate her intentions as a simple command but as an explanation, the task, as formulated by the mother at least, is to get information across to the child which the child does not yet have. It was mentioned in the text that this is one of the most difficult tasks encountered in verbal mother-child interactions, since the content is not known to the child and the code is obviously not yet well mastered. The child has therefore, so to say, to solve an equation with two unknowns. Since this is obviously impossible, as will be remembered from High School algebra, the mother does the most meaningful thing possible—she provides several or many "equations" to help the child solve the problem. Those "equations" are the repeated utterances of the mother wherein the content is closely related but the specific utterances are different. How difficult this communication task is may be seen from the fact that at the end the mother takes recourse to deixis and nonverbal modeling.

Although a single example obviously cannot be a basis for a generalization of conclusions, it still might serve as a basis for a suggestion: Both the underlying logic and the example suggest that an emphasis upon the functional use of language, whether by the mother or by the investigator, might be quite counterproductive for language transmission/acquisition and the understanding of the underlying processes, respectively. Considered from the point of skill learning, this makes eminently sense: A skill has to be mastered before it can be used effectively. If a skill/tool is not yet mastered, an attempt to simultaneously train it and utilize it effectively leads to difficulties. The training of component skills has to be reasonably advanced before they can be integrated and applied to practical tasks.

Appendix 1

# of Utt.	Child	Mother	Instructional Contents	Instructional Methods
577	Fraser cup.	Eve, why don't you drink it out of the cup?	Transf. S-V-O-PPh; Negation; Features of *drink*	06–INCORPORATION 24–MORPHEME PERSEVERATION 57–FUNCTIONAL ELABORATION
		See, F. is not drinking his coffee that way.	S-V-O-Adv.; Negation; Concord N-Aux.-Pr.	05–COMBINATORY IMITATION 25–REPLACEMENT MAJOR 28–TRANSFORMATION
		He's not drinking his coffee with his spoon.	S-V-O-PPh; Concord repeated	05–COMBINATORY IMITATION 25–REPLACEMENT MAJOR
		Drink your juice out of the cup.	V-O-PPh; Implied Pr. concord	25–REPLACEMENT MAJOR 28–TRANSFORMATION 29–VOCABULARY PERSEVERATION
		You eat with your spoon.	S-V-PPh; PPh structurally clarified; features of *eat*	25–REPLACEMENT MAJOR; 26 + 57
		No; you're getting it all over you.	S-V-O-PPh; Concord	24–MORPHEME PERSEVERATION 51–MAPPING
		Look, you're spilling it on your dress.	S-V-O-PPh; Concord; *you're* + *you your*	24–MORPHEME PERSEVERATION; 51 + 52–REPHRASING
		You drink it out of the cup.	S-V-O-PPh; Features of *drink*	25–REPLACEMENT MAJOR 26–REPLACEMENT MINOR 29–VOCABULARY PERSEVERATION
		F. drinks his coffee that way.	S-V-O-Adv.; Concord; Noun-3rd pers.-Pr.	23–BREAK DOWN; 25–REPLACEMENT MAJOR

113

Appendix 1 (cont.)

#of utt.	Child	Mother	Instructional Contents	Instructional Methods
		And Eve drinks her grape juice that way.	S-V-O-Adv.; Concord; Noun-3rd pers.-Pr.	24—MORPHEME PERSEVERATION 25—REPLACEMENT MAJOR
	Get grape juice cup.	Yes.	V-O-(PPh)	80—POSITIVE FEEDBACK
		It's in the cup right here.	Contrast; F-V vs. Cop. sent.; S-Cop.-PPh	25—COMBINATORY IMITATION 07—CHAINING 27—FRAME VARIATION
		Right here.	Deixis; Vocabulary	23—BREAK DOWN
	A spoon.	No; you don't drink grape juice with a spoon.	S-V-O-PPh; Features of *drink*; Negation transf.	06—INCORPORATION 25—REPLACEMENT MAJOR 28—TRANSFORMATION
		You drink it out of the cup.	S-V-O-PPh; Concord: *grape juice = it*	25—REPLACEMENT MAJOR; 28 + 29—VOCABULARY PERSEVERATION
	Drink coffee.	Yes.	Features of *drink*	80—POSITIVE FEEDBACK
		He's going to drink the coffee.	S-V-O; Verb Phrase more complex; Immediate future	02—EXPANSION 23—BREAK DOWN 26—REPLACEMENT MINOR
		Then I stir it.	S-V-O; Concord: *coffee = it*	51—MAPPING 58—COMPLEX ELABORATION
	Then stir it.	That's the way?	Contrast: FV vs. Cop. Sent.; *way* in new slot	27—FRAME VARIATION
		See? From the cup.	Vocabulary equivalence; *Look - see* PPh with same meaning as above but new preposition	52—REPHRASING 26—REPLACEMENT MINOR

Appendix 2 Utterances 1289 ff)

Appendix 2 contrasts in many aspects with Appendix 1. Not only is the language not used by the mother to accomplish a nonverbal goal, but even the linguistic focus of both interaction partners is different. In contrast to Appendix 1, where most or all of the vocabulary items were obviously familiar to the child and the emphasis was placed upon getting practical information across, which was mainly attempted by the syntactic/semantic combination of the known vocabulary items, in Appendix 2 the child is actively engaged in acquiring new vocabulary items. In this manner, Appendix 2 reflects one of the quite elementary tasks in the transmission/acquisition of language skills, at least as far as the child's initiative is concerned. The mother nevertheless utilizes the opportunity to add some syntactic teaching, e.g., line 1, 2, i.e., pertaining to the form of copula sentences, and repeatedly pertaining to the syntactic slot in which the newly trained words can be used (*Hot tapioca, hot water, it will be cool*). The mother's indirect correction (line 3), the repetitiveness of the training (especially *Vanilla*), and her restructuring of the child's formulaic contribution (*Hot and cool*) into a common syntactic form (. . . *it will be cool*) will be of additional theoretical interest.

Appendix 2

# of Utt.	Child	Mother	Instructional Contents	Instructional Methods
1289	That?	What is that?	Vocabulary	06–INCORPORATION 53–ASKS FOR LABEL
	Hot.	It's hot.	Cop. Sent.; Vocabulary	02–EXPANSION 29–VOCABULARY PERSEVERATION
		But what is it?	Vocabulary; Feature of *what*	20–REPETITION 81–NEGATIVE FEEDBACK 53–ASKS FOR LABEL
	Eve tapioca.	Yes.	Vocabulary	80–POSITIVE FEEDBACK
		It's hot tapioca.	Cop. Sent.; Vocabulary in its syntactic slot	02–EXPANSION; 05–COMBINATORY IMITATION 29–VOCABULARY PERSEVERATION
	Hot tapioca.			
	That?	It's hot water.	Vocabulary in its syntactic slot	25–REPLACEMENT MAJOR 29–VOCABULARY PERSEVERATION

Appendix 2 (cont.)

#of utt.	Child	Mother	Instructional Contents	Instructional Methods
	Water hot.			
	Eve tapioca hot.	Uh hum.	Vocabulary	80–POSITIVE FEEDBACK
	Hot.	Uh hum.	Vocabulary	80–POSITIVE FEEDBACK
	And cool.	And cool,	Vocabulary	01–SIMPLE IMITATION
		yes.	Vocabulary	80–POSITIVE FEEDBACK
		By the time you have lunch it will be cool.	Contrast; F-V vs. Copula sentence; vocabulary in its syntactic slot	06–INCORPORATION 22–BUILD UP
	That?	What is that?	Vocabulary	06–INCORPORATION 53–ASKS FOR LABEL
		Vanilla.	Vocabulary	50–PROVIDES LABEL
	Vanilla.	Vanilla.	Vocabulary	09–IMITATION + REPETITION 29–VOCABULARY PERSEVERATION
	Vanilla.	Vanilla.	Vocabulary	09–IMITATION + REPETITION 29–VOCABULARY PERSEVERATION

Appendix 3 (Utterances 1458ff)

Appendix 3 represents in many respects an integration of the phenomena found in Appendices 1 and 2. The goal of the verbal interaction is again very practical/functional. The mother's consistent and often repeated attempts to get her message across are fully evident. But Eve is much more actively involved in the interchange than she was in Appendix 1 (probably because the maternal input is simpler). Eve exercises actively the noun phrase with its constituents (*big one, big stool, Mom lap, Pap study, Eve stool*, etc.), picks up briefly on prepositional uses (*on Mommy lap, by me, by tape recorder, on stool*) and rehearses twice the vocabulary item *tape recorder* after her mother has modeled it four times. Less immediately obvious in its effects upon the child, but probably a very suggestive indication of the "world view" predominant in the family culture of the child, is the emphasis upon constructions containing possessive expressions. They begin with line 1 (*Mom lap, my lap*) are found repeatedly through the text, and predominate to the end (*Put your foot on your own stool; That is my stool and that belongs to you*). This clear delimitation of personal spheres might be a typical Western middle class phenomenon and would deserve specific attention, indicating a still further phenomenon of language study besides those of syntactics, semantics, and pragmatics in the commonly conceived sense. Whereas the mother utilizes both opportunities to add the *s* of the Saxon Genitive (*Pap's study, Mommy's stool*), the child does not yet pick up this little stressed morphological item. Also in other respects this episode is basically devoid of any evidence of morphological learning. This observation, together with that of Appendix 2 and several of the following ones, suggest a further possibility that seems to have largely been neglected in the available reports on child language acquisition: It appears that during specific episodes, either due to practical or instructional considerations, one specific linguistic task is focused upon and intensively rehearsed, in the form of massed training, accompanied by the relative neglect of other instructional opportunities and linguistic structures.

Appendix 3

#of utt.	Child	Mother	Instructional Contents	Instructional Methods
1458	Eve sit Mom lap.	You wanna sit on my lap?	Mod. aux.; S-V-PPh (on)	02–EXPANSION
		Oh, but I am very busy.	Cop. Sent.	02–EXPANSION 22–BUILD UP
		You can sit on my lap later.	Mod. aux.; S-V-PPh	25–REPLACEMENT MAJOR
	Eve sit on Mommy lap.	You can sit out here by me on the other stool.	S-V-Adv.-PPh (by)-PPh (on)	25–REPLACEMENT MAJOR 51–MAPPING
	By me.	Yes.		80–POSITIVE FEEDBACK
		On the stool.	PPh (on)	23–BREAK DOWN 29–VOCABULARY PERSEVERATION
		But you'd better get the big stool, Eve.	Mod. aux.; S-V-O	25–REPLACEMENT MAJOR 27–FRAME VARIATION 55–FEATURE ELABORATION
		Not the little stool, the big one.		25–REPLACEMENT MAJOR 40–CONTRASTING CORRECTION 55–FEATURE ELABORATION
	Big one.	The big one.		02–EXPANSION; 29–VOCABULARY
	The big one.	The big one, like I'm sitting on.	S-V-Prep.	29–VOCABULARY PERSEVERATION 51–MAPPING
		The big stool.		20–REPETITION 29–VOCABULARY PERSEVERATION
	A big stool.	Yes.		80–POSITIVE FEEDBACK

Appendix 3 (cont.)

#of utt.	Child	Mother	Instructional Contents	Instructional Methods
		You get the other big stool.	S-V-O	06–INCORPORATION 29–VOCABULARY PERSEVERATION 55–FEATURE ELABORATION
	A Pap study.	It's not in Pap's study.	Neg. Cop. Sent.; PPh (*in*)	06–INCORPORATION
		It's under the tape recorder.	Cop. Sent. with PPh PPh (*under*)	25–REPLACEMENT MAJOR 28–TRANSFORMATION 51–MAPPING
	The tape recorder.	I'm sorry.	Cop. Sent. with Adv.	23–BREAK DOWN
		It's not.	Neg. Cop. Sent. with Ellipsis	
		It's beside the tape recorder.	Cop. Sent. with PPh PPh (*beside*)	25–REPLACEMENT MAJOR 51–MAPPING
		Beside the tape recorder. That one.	PPh (*beside*)	23–BREAK DOWN 51–MAPPING
	That one.	No; the big stool.	*big*	20–REPETITION 29–VOCABULARY PERSEVERATION 40–CONTRASTING CORRECTION
		Like this one		51–MAPPING
		The big stool, like I'm sitting on.	*big*; S-V-Prep.	27–FRAME VARIATION 51–MAPPING 29–VOCABULARY PERSEVERATION

Appendix 3 (cont.)

#of utt.	Child	Mother	Instructional Contents	Instructional Methods
	Eve stool.	Right by the tape recorder.	PPh (*by*)	21–COMPLETION 25–REPLACEMENT MAJOR 51–MAPPING
	Right tape recorder.	The big stool.		23–BREAK DOWN 29–VOCABULARY PERSEVERATION
	Big stool.	Right.		80–POSITIVE FEEDBACK
	By tape recorder.	That one.		51–MAPPING
	That a one. The banjo.	I know it's your banjo.	Contrast: F–V vs. Cop. Sentence	02–EXPANSION 29–VOCABULARY PERSEVERATION
	Come back.	There. Are you gonna sit down on the stool?	Transf. S–V–PPh PPh (*on*)	25–REPLACEMENT MAJOR 29–VOCABULARY PERSEVERATION
	Eve sit down.	Well, this is my stool.	Cop. Sent.	27–FRAME VARIATION 51–MAPPING 29–VOCABULARY PERSEVERATION
		You sit on the other side.	S–V–PPh; PPh (*on*)	25–REPLACEMENT MAJOR 28–TRANSFORMATION
	Mommy stool.	This is Mommy's stool.	Cop. Sent.	02–EXPANSION 51–MAPPING 29–VOCABULARY PERSEVERATION

Possessive Morphemes ⟶

Appendix 3 (cont.)

#of utt.	Child	Mother	Instructional Contents	Instructional Methods
......		Right.		80–POSITIVE FEEDBACK
		Will you please sit on your stool?	V-PPh (on)	25–REPLACEMENT MAJOR
		You're in my way.	Cop. Sent.; PPh (in)	27–FRAME VARIATION 51–MAPPING
		Please sit on your stool.	PPh (on)	23–BREAK DOWN 28–TRANSFORMATION
	On stool. Mommy way.	You're in my way.	Cop. Sent.; PPh (in)	02–EXPANSION 20–REPETITION
		Yes.		
		Put your foot on your own stool.	V-O-PPh; PPh (on)	25–REPLACEMENT MAJOR 29–VOCABULARY PERSEVERATION
	Own stool.	That's right.	Cop. Sent.	80–POSITIVE FEEDBACK
		That is my stool and that belongs to you.	Cop. Sent.	02–EXPANSION 29–VOCABULARY PERSEVERATION

Appendix 4 (Utterances 2868 ff)

After the emphasis upon massed training in the discussion of Appendix 3, the reason for the selection of this episode is quite self-evident. The episode is presented as an example of spaced rehearsal. The topic is, of course, that of Appendix 1, encountered some two thousand utterances previously, which arises again in the course of the everyday activities in the home. Fascinating phenomena can be observed in this brief interaction: First, Eve has evidently learned something from one of the previous pertinent interactions, since she begins the episode with the construction *out milk bottle*. It will be remembered that in Appendix 1 the mother had repeatedly used the prepositional phrase *out of . . . .* The mother on her part seems to remember the past communicational difficulties, since she begins immediately with her intensive reformulations of the message as described in connection with Appendix 1. But she has forgotten one aspect of the previous episode, namely that she employed the construction *out of . . . .* Now she employs the construction *from . . .*, which seems to present for Eve a too demanding alternation. Only after Eve has repeated twice constructions employing *out of . . .* does her mother catch on to the discrepancy and switches to *out of . . .*, not without coming back in the last utterance of the episode to the construction with *from . . . (from your cup)*. Such cyclic phenomena—both as they are found after longer intervals of thousands of utterances and as encountered here, with one construction being employed at the beginning and end of one single episode—have been repeatedly encountered in the interactions of Eve and her mother; they make very much sense learning theoretically, considering primacy and recency effects as well as the importance of spaced rehearsal. They appear to deserve specific attention, especially since most of the commonly employed methodologies, including those of the present study, would lead to their being overlooked.

Appendix 4

# of Utt	Child	Mother	Instructional Contents	Instructional Methods
2868	Baby S. drink out milk bottle.	Oh, is she?	V-S Question; N-Pr Equiv.; Concord; Aux.	02–EXPANSION 28–TRANSFORMATION
		That's because she is a baby.	2 Cop. Sent.; Contrast; Aux. vs copula *is*	27–FRAME VARIATION 28–TRANSFORMATION
		Babies drink from bottles.	S-V-PPh; Plural	27–FRAME VARIATION
		Big people drink from cups.	S-V-PPh; Plural	
		I drink my milk from a cup.	S-V-O-PPh; Contrast; drink V_i vs V_t	22–BUILD UP 25–REPLACEMENT MAJOR
		I drink my beer from a cup too.	S-V-O-PPh; Article with count noun	22–BUILD UP 25–REPLACEMENT MAJOR
	I drink out grape juice from cup.			
	He drink coffee out cup.	Sure.	Reward for approximation to PPh	80–POSITIVE FEEDBACK
		And Mommy drinks coffee out of a cup too.	Concord; PPh with familiar Prep.; S-V-O-PPh	02–EXPANSION 09–IMITATION + REPETITION 26–REPLACEMENT MINOR
		When you are big you drink out of a cup.	Contrast; Cop. vs. F-V Sent; Complex Sent.; *drink* as V_i; S-V-PPh	25–REPLACEMENT MAJOR 52–REPHRASING 58–COMPLEX ELABORATION
		Look at this big girl drink out of a cup.	Complex Sent.; *drink* as V_i; S-V-PPh	22–BUILD UP 25–REPLACEMENT MAJOR
		Look at that.	Analysis of complex sent.	23–BREAK DOWN
2890	.... (I) drinking.	You drink from your cup.	S-V-PPh; Reinstatement of *from*; Analysis of complex sentence	

Appendix 5

Appendix 5 is obviously an episode in which the irregular past of the auxiliaries is the predominant subject. It is modeled intensively by the mother, basically in each of her utterances, but not yet imitated by the child, besides the phrase *had supper* which she employs without a preceding model. Also of interest is the fact that, in this conversation of past experiences, Eve is relatively reticent and the mother has to contribute most of the conversation. This is especially precarious for the mother, since in this case her questions are genuine questions for information and the child has to contribute the information. We find, therefore, a strong emphasis upon questions asked by the mother in order to elicit the contributions of Eve. The mother also repeats the child's answers partially or fully, probably to add substance to the conversation, but at the same time providing models of complete syntactic constructions and of the syntactic relationships or contrasts between interrogative and affirmative sentences. The reader is again referred to rhythmic patterns: *did you . . ., were they . . ., you were . . ., did you . . ., you had . . ., did you . . ., you did . . ., did you . . .,* which partly repeat the cyclic phenomenon discussed in connection with Appendix 4.

Appendix 5

# of Utt.	Child	Mother	Instructional Contents		Instructional Methods
5355	....	Did you have fun playing outside this morning?	Irreg. Past: *do*		27–FRAME VARIATION
		What were you doing?	Irreg. Past: *be*; Concord: *they - were*	⎱ 2 quest. forms	24–MORPHEME PERSEVERATION 54–ASKS FOR VERB
	Putting sand in the pail.	Putting sand in the pail?			01–SIMPLE IMITATION
		You were?	Irreg. Past: *be*	Concord; *you-were* 2 quest. forms	08–TWO PERSON SENTENCE 24–MORPHEME PERSEVERATION 28–TRANSFORMATION
		What else did you do?	Irreg. Past: *do*	*did you*	22–BUILD UP; 24–MORPHEME PERS.

Appendix 5 (cont.)

#of utt.	Child	Mother	Instructional Contents	Instructional Methods
	Had supper.			54—ASKS FOR VERB 28—TRANSFORMATION
		Oh, you had supper.	Irreg. Past: *have you had*	02—EXPANSION 24—MORPHEME PERSEVERATION 28—TRANSFORMATION
		What did you eat?	Irreg. Past: *do did you*	24—MORPHEME PERSEVERATION 25—REPLACEMENT MAJOR 61—ITEM SPECIFICATION 28—TRANSFORMATION
	Macaroni.			
		Oh, you did.	Irreg. Past: *do you did*	08—TWO PERSON SENTENCE 24—MORPHEME PERSEVERATION 28—TRANSFORMATION
		Did you cook it?	Irreg. Past: *do did you*	24—MORPHEME PERSEVERATION 27—FRAME VARIATION 56—ACTION ELABORATION 28—TRANSFORMATION

Appendix 6

In the same manner as Appendix 5 focused upon the irregular past, Appendix 6 could be labeled a lesson in personal pronouns. Within around one page of text, that is, within approximately four minutes of conversation, six out of the eight personal pronouns are used, and used repeatedly. When the adult employs the personal pronouns, an exercise in concord between the pronouns and the verbs is almost necessarily involved, and in some cases the personal pronouns are juxtaposed to possessive ones. Since the personal pronouns are used to refer to either designata present in the setting or to clearly named absent persons, their deictic function is relatively easily discernible. Since the designans-designatum relationship is mostly repeated several times, the child also has ample opportunity to recognize this relationship from the multiple juxtapositions of label and referent.

Besides these major aspects of the interaction, two minor phenomena shall be mentioned, since they may easily escape the attention of the casual reader and since they appear to be of some theoretical and practical importance, respectively: First, although it follows logically from many of the prior observations that Eve often catches on to phenomena only after several repetitions in the maternal speech, it deserves emphasis how potentially misleading formulations of the mother, appearing only once, leave no trace in Eve's verbal behavior. When the mother says: *"She's sleeping up in her bed."*, the sequence *up in* could easily be taken as a composite preposition in parallel fashion to the one encountered in Appendices 4 and 1, *out of*. But to the assurance of the psycholinguists who were concerned about the possible negative influence of adult disfluences and mistakes, it can be seen that Eve completely disregards this single construction, even though the utterance was an answer to her question and she seems to be taking account of the content of this answer. In contrast to this disregard of the form of the input stand the next two utterances. Whereas the mother addresses Fraser in her remark about the cream pitcher, Eve picks up on the mother's remark and her action and she comments upon them. This observation suggests that the often emphasized phenomenon that young children attend only to the input directed towards themselves has to be taken with some caution. It may fully apply to the very young child in the very first stages of language development, but it does not exclusively apply anymore to Eve when she is around 27 months old and has progressed to relatively advanced speech. At these later stages, children may pick up information from overheard speech when it is accompanied by nonverbally structured information that helps to disambiguate it. This suggestion might be of considerable importance for language instruction in nursery school, educational TV shows, and any multiple listener situation. Considering these practical applications, it appears worthwhile to pay special attention to this phenomenon in some future studies.

Appendix 6

# of Utt.	Child	Mother	Instructional Contents	Instructional Methods
10024	Where (are) you, S??	I'm right here.	*You;I;* Concord; Pr.-Cop.	28–TRANSFORMATION
		Where are you?	*You;* Concord;	04–SUBST. IMITATION 24–MORPHEME PERSEVERATION 61–ITEM SPECIFICATION
			(Simple present Cop.)	
	This not straight.	It's not straight.	*it;* Concord; Pr.–Cop.	02–EXPANSION
		I know it's not straight.	*I; it*	02–EXPANSION 20–REPETITION
	Where Sarah?	She's sleeping up in her bed.	*She;* Concord; Cop. + Poss. Pr.; Pres. Prog	28–TRANSFORMATION 56–ELABORATION
		I broke my cream pitcher so I'll just give it to you. (Mother to Fraser as she pours milk)	*I;* Concord; Poss. Pr.; *I, it, you;* Irr. Past + Fut.	25–REPLACEMENT MAJOR
	There some cream.			07–CHAINING 27–FRAME VARIATION 51–MAPPING
	Put it in you coffee.			27–FRAME VARIATION 51–MAPPING
.....	get your(s) out.	Ok, I'll get mine out (Fraser).	Poss. Pr. absolute form + Fut.	24–MORPHEME PERSEVERATION 25–REPLACEMENT MAJOR 28–TRANSFORMATION
	I use this one (n) you use that one.			25–REPLACEMENT MAJOR 26–REPLACEMENT MINOR

Appendix 6 (cont.)

#of utt.	Child	Mother	Instructional Contents	Instructional Methods
	I using Fraser's, Fraser using mine(s).			23–BREAK DOWN 26–REPLACEMENT MINOR 27–FRAME VARIATION
		He is?	He; Concord	02–EXPANSION 41–CHALLENGE
	Ready to turn it.			
		Are we? Not quite.	We; Concord	24–MORPHEME PERSEVERATION 41–CHALLENGE
		We're not quite ready to turn the page (Fraser).	We; Concord + Negation	07–CHAINING 24–MORPHEME PERSEVERATION 28–TRANSFORMATION
	Yep we are.		We; Concord	24–MORPHEME PERSEVERATION 28–TRANSFORMATION
		We what? (Fraser)	We;	07–CHAINING 61–SPECIFICATION
	Yep we are, Fraser.		We; Concord	20–REPETITION 24–MORPHEME PERSEVERATION 28–TRANSFORMATION
		Nope, not yet, E. (Fraser)		
	Yes, but you can't go.		You + Negation	23–BREAK DOWN 24–MORPHEME PERSEVERATION
	Did you make a great big hole in here? (To mother)		You + Question + Irreg. Past	24–MORPHEME PERSEVERATION 25–REPLACEMENT MAJOR 51–MAPPING

Appendix 6 (cont.)

#of utt.	Child	Mother	Instructional Contents	Instructional Methods
		Yes, we made a great big hole in here;	*We* + Irr. Past	24-MORPHEME PERSEVERATION 28-TRANSFORMATION 80-POSITIVE FEEDBACK
		We have to get a new one.	*We* + Model Aux.	25-REPLACEMENT MAJOR 27-FRAME VARIATION
	S., I want have my lunch.		*I* + Modal Aux.	25-REPLACEMENT MAJOR 26-REPLACEMENT MINOR
		But it's not time for lunch, yet.	*It*; Concord + Neg.	27-FRAME VARIATION
		You wait just a little bit and we'll have lunch.	*You; We;* Fut.	27-FRAME VARIATION 24-MORPHEME PERSEVERATION 04-SUBSTITUTING IMITATION
	(Want) some lunch.			23-BREAK DOWN 26-REPLACEMENT MINOR
		Not now.	*I*	23-BREAK DOWN
	I want some.			22-BUILD UP 23-BREAK DOWN
		Not now, it's not time.	*It*; Concord + Neg.	22-BUILD UP 23-BREAK DOWN

Appendix 7

Appendix 7 contains one full hour of interactions between Eve and her mother, together with some of the analyses performed on these interactions. To comment exhaustively on it in microanalytical approaches could easily fill an entire separate monograph. A somewhat abbreviated interpretation will be prepared for future publication. At the present moment, this hour of interactions is only presented as an example of the phenomena observable and of the way they have been analyzed by employing the categories of Instructional Methods described in the monograph. The analysis of the Instructional Contents shall again indicate how rich in linguistic information these interactions are. Even a cursory glance at this latter analysis will indicate clearly that the summarized points by far do not exhaust the information the child could have abstracted from the interactions. As indicated in the main body of the study, the total amount of linguistic information provided for the child within even a single hour of interactions easily approaches several ten thousand items. With such a wealth of well structured information available, it might not be astonishing that an intelligent and well motivated child could learn many linguistic skills in relatively brief time spans.

Appendix 7

1 Hour of Speech Input: Its Instructional Value and Interactional Function

# of Utt.	Child	Mother	Instructional Contents	Instructional Methods
1	More cookie.			
2		You . . . more cookies?	S-V-O; Plural	02–EXPANSION
3		How about another graham cracker?	Vocabulary equivalences	25–REPLACEMENT FULL
7	More cookie.			
8		You have another cookie right on the table.	S-V-O; Determ. - Noun Prep.-Art-Noun	06–INCORPORATION 25–REPLACEMENT FULL 51–MAPPING
9	More juice?			
10		More juice?		
11		Would you like more grape juice?	Transf. S-V-O; Determ. - Noun	06–INCORPORATION 22–BUILD-UP
14	Fraydiy.			
15		I think that was "Fraser."	Phonetic	01–SIMPLE IMITATION
16		I'm not sure.	Contrast: Full - Verb vs. Copula Sentence	27–FRAME VARIATION
17	Fraydiy.			
18		What?	Phonetics	01–IMITATION
19		Are you saying "Fraser?"	Phonetics	02–EXPANSION
20		Mr. Fraser?		
21	Fraydee.			
22		Yes.	Phonetics	80–POSITIVE FEEDBACK
23		That's much better	Phonetics	80–POSITIVE FEEDBACK
22	Fraydeee.			
25		Mr. Fraser?	Phonetics	02–EXPANSION
26	Yeah.			

Appendix 7 (cont.)

#of utt.	Child	Mother	Instructional Contents	Instructional Methods
42	Telephone.			
43		Well, go and get your telephone.	V-V-O; Possess.	06–INCORPORATION 25–REPLACEMENT FULL
44		Yes.		
45		He gave you your telephone.	S-V-IO-DO; Possess	06–INCORPORATION 25–REPLACEMENT FULL
46		Who are you calling, Eve?	Transf. S-V-O	57–FUNCTIONAL ELABORATION
47	My telephone.			
48		Who?	Dist. Feature of Pronoun	23–BREAK DOWN 61–ITEM SPECIFICATION
49	More . . . cookie.			
63				
64		You want cookie?	S-V-O, Request Verb	06–INCORPORATION
65		There's a cookie on the table. In the room, on the table with the rest of your crackers.	Contrast: -F-V vs. Cop. Sentence 5 times Prep. - Deter - Noun with substitutions; Plural	06–INCORPORATION 27–FRAME VARIATION 51–MAPPING
71	Mommy read.			
72		No.		
73		Mommy can't read.	Transf. S-V	28–TRANSFORMATION
74		I'm busy.	Contrast; F-V vs. Cop. Sentence	27–FRAME VARIATION 22–BUILD UP
75		You read the book.	S-V-O; 2 Syntactic Forms of *read*	25–REPLACEMENT FULL 28–TRANSFORMATION
76	A stool.			
77		Yes.	Vocabulary	80–POSITIVE FEEDBACK 04–IMITATION WITH SUBSTITUTION
78		That's the stool.	Cop. sentence; Vocabulary	06–INCORPORATION 50–PROVIDES LABEL

Appendix 7 (cont.)

#of utt.	Child	Mother	Instructional Contents	Instructional Methods
79		You want to sit on the stool and read the book?	Contrast; Cop. vs. F-V sentence + PPh Vocabulary, Contrast; V_i vs V_t	06–INCORPORATION 57–FUNCTIONAL ELABORATION 27–FRAME VARIATION
80	Fraser.	Mr. Fraser.	Phonetics	02–EXPANSION; 20–REPETITION 80–POSITIVE FEEDBACK
81		Yes.	Phonetics	02–EXPANSION
82		Mr. Fraser.	Phonetics	20–REPETITION
83				
84	Fraser.			
85	More cookie.			
86		Your cookie's there on the table.	Transf. from #65; PPhs (#8,65,79,86)	06–INCORPORATION 27–FRAME VARIATION 51–MAPPING
87		Did you eat it?	Transf. S-V-O; Contrast; Cop. vs. F-V sentence; Past Aux.	27–FRAME VARIATION
88		Yes.		
89		You ate it.	S-V-O; Past F-V	28–TRANSFORMATION; 24–MORPH. PERSEV. 29–VOCABULARY PERSEVERATION
90		I'll give you another.	S-V-IO-DO; Vocabulary	29–VOCABULARY PERSEVERATION
91		Just a little one.	Vocabulary; Det. - Adj. Pr.	55–FEATURE ELABORATION
92		Just a little one.	Vocabulary; Det. - Adj. Pr.	20–REPETITION
93	Little.			55–FEATURE ELABORATION

Appendix 7 (cont.)

#of utt.	Child	Mother	Instructional Contents	Instructional Methods
94		Yes.	Vocabulary	80–POSITIVE FEEDBACK
95		Little one.	Vocabulary; NPh	02–EXPANSION; 09–IM + REP 23–BREAK DOWN
96		Yes.	Vocabulary	80–POSITIVE FEEDBACK
102		You . . . eat any more crackers.	S-V-O; Indef. Pr.; Plural	24–MORPHEME PERSEVERATION
103	Milk.			
104		Milk?		
105		No.		
106		You don't want milk, honey.	Transf. S-V-O	06–INCORPORATION 25–REPLACEMENT FULL
107		You've just had some juice.	S-V-O; Indef. Pr.	25–REPLACEMENT FULL 28–TRANSFORMATION 29–VOCABULARY PERSEVERATION
108		Where's the rest of your juice? . . .	PPh	27–FRAME VARIATION + 28
109		How about a drink of water?		25–REPLACEMENT FULL
110	That?			
111		What is that?	Vocabulary	06–INCORPORATION
112		That's Mr. Fraser.	Cop. Sent.; Phonetics ·	06 + 28 + 50 PROVIDES LABEL
113		There drink the water.	V-O, *drink* as Verb vs.#109	27–FRAME VARIATION 28–TRANSFORMATION
114	Fraser water?			
115		No.		
116		I don't think Mr. Fraser wants any water.	Complex S-V-O; NPh vs. #113	02–EXPANSION 29–VOCABULARY PERSEVERATION

Appendix 7 (cont.)

#of utt.	Child	Mother	Instructional Contents	Instructional Methods
117	Oh Fraser.			
118		What....?		
119	Bye.			
120		Bye?		
121		Where are you going?	Transf. S-V vs. Transf. Cop. Sent. (#108)	52–REPHRASING
122	. . . water.			
123	Fraser water.	Will you ask Mr. Fraser	Transf. Complex S-V-O	02–EXPANSION
124		if he'd like a drink of water?	drink as noun; PPh	Combination of #109 + #116
125				
126	Fraser water.			
127		I don't think so.	Transf. S-V	23–BREAK DOWN / 25–REPLACEMENT FULL / 51–MAPPING
128		Mr. Fraser has coffee.	S-V-O	27–FRAME VARIATION
129		Mr. Fraser's drinking coffee.	S-V-O	51–MAPPING
130	That?			
131		What is that?	Vocabulary	06–INCORPORATION / 53–ASKS FOR LABEL
132		Coffee.	Vocabulary	50–PROVIDES LABEL
133	Coffee.			
134		Yes.	Vocabulary	80–POSITIVE FEEDBACK
135		He's drinking his coffee.	S-V-O; Possess.	06–INCORPORATION / 22–BUILD UP + 51–MAPPING
136	. . . Fraser coffee.			
137		Right.	Vocabulary	80–POSITIVE FEEDBACK

Appendix 7 (cont.)

#of utt.	Child	Mother	Instructional Contents	Instructional Methods
138		That's Mr. Fraser's coffee.	Saxon Gen.; Contrast; F-V vs. Cop. Sent.	02–EXPANSION 27–FRAME VARIATION 51–MAPPING
139	Down.			
140		You want down?	Adverb S-V-Adv. positions Adv.-S-V	06–INCORPORATION
141		There you go.		27–FRAME VARIATION
142		Now what?		
143	Cookie.			
144		No more cookies, Eve.	Plural	02–EXPANSION
145		Later we'll have a cookie.	Adv.-S-V-O	06–INCORPORATION 25–REPLACEMENT FULL 27–FRAME VARIATION
146		We'll have a cookie later.	Adverb S-V-O-Adv. positions	
156	Hat.			
157		Your hat?	Possess.; Det. + N	02–EXPANSION
158		An' what did you do with it?	Past Aux.; PPh; Transf. S-V-O	06–INCORPORATION 54–ASKS FOR VERB PHRASE
172	Fraser hat.			
173	Oh Fraser hat.			
174		What?		60–REQUESTS REPETITION
175	Oh Fraser hat.			
176		I don't know what you're saying about the hat.	Det. + N; Vocabulary	02–EXPANSION 27–FRAME VARIATION 29–VOCABULARY PERSEVERATION

Appendix 7 (cont.)

#of utt	Child	Mother	Instructional Contents	Instructional Methods
177		What about the hat?	Det. + N; Vocabulary	23–BREAK DOWN 29–VOCABULARY PERSEVERATION 61–ITEM SPECIFICATION
178	Fraser hat.			
179		Oh, Mr. Fraser's hat.	Sax. Gen.; Vocabulary	02–EXPANSION 29–VOCABULARY PERSEVERATION
180		Mr. Fraser doesn't have a hat.	Transf. S-V-O; Possess; Vocabulary	06–INCORPORATION 27–FRAME VARIATION 29–VOCABULARY PERSEVERATION
181		He doesn't have a hat.	S-V-O; Possess; Vocabulary	20–REPETITION + 27 + 29 28–TRANSFORMATION 29–VOCABULARY PERSEVERATION
182		Would he like to have Eve's hat?	Transf. S-V-O; Possess; Vocabulary	
186	Eye.			
187		What's wrong with your eye?	Trans. Cop. Sent.; PPh	06–INCORPORATION
197	Soldier.			
198		Yes.	Vocabulary	80–POSITIVE FEEDBACK
199		There's soldiers on the radio.	Vocabulary; Plural; PPh	51–MAPPING + 06
200		There's two soldiers.	Vocabulary; Plural	22–BUILD UP + 51 23–BREAK DOWN
201	Solder.			
202		Soldiers.	Vocabulary	02–EXPANSION 23–BREAK DOWN
203		Uh huh.	Vocabulary	80–POSITIVE FEEDBACK 22–BUILD UP
204		Two soldiers.	Vocabulary; Plural	23–BREAK DOWN

Appendix 7 (cont.)

#of utt.	Child	Mother	Instructional Contents	Instructional Methods
205		Bring it here.		
206	That.			
207		What's that?	Vocabulary	06–INCORPORATION
208		That's Jack and Jill.	Vocabulary	50–PROVIDES LABEL
209	Fraser hat.			06–INCORPORATION
210		Mr. Fraser doesn't have a hat, darling.	Transf. S-V-O; Possess.	27.–FRAME VARIATION
				29–VOCABULARY PERSEVERATION
211		He doesn't have a hat.	Transf. S-V-O; *Fraser - he*	20–REPETITION
				29–VOCABULARY PERSEVERATION
212		Eve has a hat.	S-V-O	25–REPLACEMENT FULL + 27
				28–TRANSFORMATION + 29
221	Man.			
222		Man?	Vocabulary	01–SIMPLE IMITATION
223		Who is that man?	Who - Cop. Sent.	06–INCORPORATION
				22–BUILD UP; 53–ASKS LABEL
224	Eve.			
225		Eve?		01–SIMPLE IMITATION
				41–CHALLENGE
226		You're Eve.	Cop. Sent.	50–PROVIDES LABEL
227		What's that man's name?	What - Cop. Sent.	06–INCORPORATION
				53–ASKS LABEL
				27.–FRAME VARIATION
231	That.			
232		That'll keep you busy.	Vocabulary	06–INCORPORATION

Appendix 7 (cont.)

#of utt.	Child	Mother	Instructional Contents	Instructional Methods
233	Busy.			
234		Busy.	Vocabulary	01–SIMPLE IMITATION 23–BREAK DOWN + 29
235		Yes.	Vocabulary	80–POSITIVE FEEDBACK
236		That'll keep you busy.	Vocabulary	09–IMITATION + REPETITION 22–BUILD UP + 29
237	Busy.			
238		Yes.	Vocabulary	80–POSITIVE FEEDBACK 20–REPETITION
239		That'll keep Eve busy.	Vocabulary; Pron-Name Equiv.	29–VOCABULARY PERSEVERATION 27–FRAME VARIATION
240	Man a pencil.	There you write a letter.	S-V-O	
241	Man a pencil.			
242		What about the pencil?	Def. vs. Indef. Article	61–ITEM SPECIFICATION
243	Man a pencil.			
244		OK 'man a pencil.		01–SIMPLE IMITATION 29–VOCABULARY PERSEVERATION
245		No.		81–NEGATIVE FEEDBACK
246		That's Eve's pencil.	Sax. Gen. Possess., Cop. Sent.	02–EXPANSION; 22–BUILD UP 25–REPLACEMENT FULL
247		That's your pencil.	Possess. Pr., Cop. Sent.	20–REPETITION + 02 + 25
248		You write with it.	S-V; write V$_i$; PPh	27–FRAME VARIATION; 57– FUNCTIONAL ELABORATION
249	Man.			
250		The man's writing with his pencil.	Possess. Pr.; PPh	06–INCORPORATION; 51–MAPPING 25–REPLACEMENT FULL

Appendix 7 (cont.)

#of utt.	Child	Mother	Instructional Contents	Instructional Methods
251	Pencil.			
252	Eve pencil.			
253	Man a pencil.			
254	Pencil.			
256	Man.			
269	Shoe.			
270	Yes.			
271		There's lots of shoes in that book.	Cop. Sent.; Plural; PPh	06–INCORPORATION 51–MAPPING
272	Shoe.			
273		What is that?	Vocabulary	53–ASKS FOR LABEL
274		Yes.	Vocabulary	80–POSITIVE FEEDBACK
275		Shoe.	Vocabulary	09–IMITATION + REPETITION 29–VOCABULARY PERSEVERATION
276	Shoe.			
277	My.			
278		Your what?	Possess. Pr.	61–ITEM SPECIFICATION
279	Mommy book.			
280		Mommy's book?	Sax. Gen. Possess.	02–EXPANSION 41–CHALLENGE
281		No.	Possess.	81–NEGATIVE FEEDBACK
282		That's Eve's book.	Cop. Sent.; Sax. Gen. Possess.	22–BUILD UP 25–REPLACEMENT FULL

Appendix 7 (cont.)

#of utt.	Child	Mother	Instructional Contents	Instructional Methods
289	Read?			
290		No.		
291		Mommy's not gonna read.	Transf. S-V	06–INCORPORATION
292		Eve read book.	S-V-O *read* $V_i + V_t$	22–BUILD UP 25–REPLACEMENT FULL 28–TRANSFORMATION
293		You read the book.	S-V-O	22–BUILD UP
294	Rackety-Boom.			
295	Read?			
296		No.		
297		Mommy can't read.	Transf. S-V; *read*— V_i; Aux.	06–INCORPORATION 28–TRANSFORMATION
298		Mommy's busy.	Contrast, Cop. vs. F-V Sent.	29–FRAME VARIATION 23–BREAK DOWN
299		Eve read.	Contrast; S-V vs. Cop. Sent.	28–TRANSFORMATION 25–REPLACEMENT FULL
300	Read choo-choo.			

The Best Mothers Are Functional: A Commentary

Donald M. Baer
The University of Kansas

Language acquisition has long been a strategic problem. Linguists always have studied how people spoke here and there, ostensibly in terms of what was different here from there, but strategically in terms of what was the same everywhere. Of course, in that context, the acquisition of those communalities would quickly become a central problem; and the declaration that the communalities of language are in fact universal necessities would be a tempting tactical solution: they are acquired because they have to be. Suitably mandatory acquisition mechanisms could be invented (and were).

Similarly, psychologists always have studied how behavior is acquired, ostensibly in terms of the variety of mechanisms that seem to be involved, but strategically in terms of how few mechanisms they might be reduced to when analyzed. Of course, in that context, the possibility that the apparent variety of behavior-acquisition mechanisms are in fact only complex variants and superstructures of the primitive reinforcement, punishment, and extinction contingencies would be a tempting tactical solution: you can find in almost any behavior's environment what look like the contingencies that established it and now support it (or now discourage it).

To put psychologists and linguists in interaction, all that was needed was an equation of language to behavior. The equation of language to behavior allowed psychologists to attempt the analysis of language acquisition (especially first-language acquisition); it also allows linguists to argue that psychologists must not yet understand a great deal about *human* behavior, probably because they have too long neglected the acquisition of language as the most strategic case in point of them all. It urges linguists to learn something about the analysis of behavior other than language, and urges psychologists to learn something about the analysis of language as other than behavior. It confronts psychologists with the demand to be logical thoroughly enough to account for a more complex and more comprehensive set of relationships than they have been accustomed to before; and it confronts linguists with the demand to prove their apparently factual assertions about language more thoroughly than they have been accustomed to before. And it generates some new researchers—students of both kinds of argument, trained in the logic and methods of both (although usually not in equitable balance), who might as well be (and are) called psycholinguists.

In the report that follows, one psycholinguist's conclusions about the nature of language acquisition are challenged by another psycholinguist's different analysis of the same data. The first listened extensively to the language interactions of a mother and her daughter, and doubted that those interactions constituted cause (on the mother's side) of the language-acquisition effects (on the daughter's side). The second read the first's data, and applied to it rather more of the psychologists' potential contributions:

(a) most important, a knowledge of what teaching contingencies can and do look like, especially in the variety that characterizes everyday human interaction, behavior control, and teaching (deliberate and inadvertent), and especially in the forms that have been proven experimentally to be effective behavior-changing contingencies;

(b) out of that knowledge, a provisional system of mother-child language interaction categories that represent most of that variety, and are observable, denotable, and countable by well trained but still quite ordinary observers;

(c) in the realization of that knowledge as data, a use of simple yet demanding procedures to evaluate whether the categorization of that mother-child interaction was done reliably, dependably, and repeatably, such that its subsequent counting was meaningful;

(d) in the reduction of those counts into dependencies and rates of dependencies that quantified mother-child interaction into its putative teaching-and-learning patterns, a knowledge of probability and conditional probability, and of its evaluation as reflective of chance or of something more systematic than that, so that any systematic effect could be appreciated as such; and

(e) the conventions for arraying those rates to show whether the mother-child interaction did after all represent a picture of possible cause and effect: of a mother plausibly teaching her daughter to acquire the mother's language.

These five contributions to the problem are typical of what is possible in psycholinguistics, but just now is being achieved as an exemplar of the discipline, its research, and its possible knowledge. Thus it is not only useful, but especially admirable, and anyone who has read this far will do far better to read much further, to Professor Moerk's last page. Nevertheless, there is a sixth element that conceivably could have been added as well, and would have represented psychology's finest contribution to the problem of language acquisition: a functional proof that certain elements of the mother's behavior were the causes of certain elements of her daughter's language.

A functional proof of teaching is the kind of proof that results when a certain aspect of the teacher's behavior is brought under experimental control, such that it happens or does not happen according to the dictates of an experimental design, rather than because of any other cause. If that is done—if an element of putative teaching behavior is made to occur sometimes but prevented from occurring at other times, and if what it purports to be teaching is learned then (or systematically later), but is not learned otherwise (at least, is not learned systematically otherwise), then we have a proof that this teaching has caused that learning. If teaching-behavior A purports to convey learned-behavior a, and teaching-behavior B purports to convey learned-behavior b, and C c, and D d, etc., a functional proof will be seen if a is acquired systematically only when A is allowed to occur, and b is acquired systematically only when B is allowed to occur, and c when C, and d when D, etc. But this will constitute a functional proof only if the occurrences of A, B, C, D, etc. are thoroughly under experimental control, and so occur only at those typically random moments when the experimental design, in its arbitrariness, has decreed that they shall.

Absent a functional proof that teacher taught student, there remains the possibility that dependencies in the behavior of the putative teacher and the putative student do not represent teacher teaching student, but instead represent student teaching teacher, or some common agent (Their Environment) teaching one or both of them to interdepend. For example, it is quite likely that when this daughter sneezes, her mother promptly and consistently says something like "God bless you!" This has the form of a reinforcement contingency, but almost certainly does not have the function of one: The daughter does not sneeze because in the past the mother subsequently has said "God bless you!"; the daughter almost surely sneezes for other reasons. Yet it would be possible to observe a mother-daughter dyad over a considerable span of time, discover that the daughter's sneezing rate is rising (perhaps she is entering the season for colds, or perhaps she is growing into an allergy), and note that her mother is pursuing her relentlessly with pseudo-reinforcing blessings for almost every sneeze. Were this a reinforcement contingency, this pattern is exactly what should be observed, and yet almost certainly this is not a reinforcement contingency. Worse yet: in the early stages of a daughter's life, the mother may not yet have learned her sneezing pattern, and thus may offer "God bless you!" 's after one or a few sneezes, only to find that several more will occur (and require further "God bless you!" 's). With experience, the mother may discover that her daughter usually sneezes in bursts of, say, four to six, and may learn to wait for the end of the burst, perhaps discriminating inter-sneeze intervals and offering the "God bless you!" only after the unusually long post-sneeze interval that marks the end of a burst. Observation of that development, which is totally a daughter-teaches-mother interaction, easily could lead an unwary nonfunctional analyst into the conclusion that the mother has shaped longer sneezing bursts in her child than the child came with. But here the child is her mother's teacher in respect to when to say "God bless you!", and someone else is the mother's teacher in respect to the whole rather silly convention of saying anything at all in response to a sneeze.

These are the kinds of interactions that merely observational systems of analyzing interdependencies may interpret as teaching interdependencies, yet (as the example shows) some of them are not, and others of them represent a different direction of who is teaching whom than the observer may suspect. Thus, the final contribution that an experimental psychology may offer to psycholinguistics is the logic and technique of a functional proof. Clearly, that option was not open to Professor Moerk in the study that follows; his reanalysis proceeded from already recorded data from interactions that only long ago were real. Thus, he has done the best that he could with the case in hand, and even so has realized a strong contribution to the question of language acquisition by this daughter in interaction with her mother: Cause-and-effect possibilities previously denied (very influentially) now are open again, and, indeed, plausible. But, in some future case (perhaps tomorrow), a functional proof may be thought of *before* it is too late to design and apply its procedures, and may be seen as impossible to harm the child involved, and so may be pursued. Professor Moerk's study is at the edges of the field today; its importance is not only its substantive conclusions but its implicit demonstration that it lacks only one element to push that edge so much farther that his present study would then be left well behind. Few studies are done at the very edges of their disciplines; fewer studies immediately clarify how to make themselves virtually obsolete by the next study. Perhaps his has achieved this because, as he says, it freely borrows from ". . . the various cognitive, social learning, ethological, and even behavioristic schools." Behaviorists in particular will see it as a useful, easily acceptable exercise in post hoc behavior analysis—how fortunate that he did not borrow from any of the odd behavioristic schools.

Response to Dr. Baer's Commentary

Ernst L. Moerk

Being told that one's work is "an exemplar of the discipline" and that it stands "at the edge of the field today" is very gratifying. I am also grateful for Dr. Baer's positive remarks concerning the methods I have employed and, of course, for the fact that he took upon himself the task of studying the rather extensive analyses I have presented.

Being very appreciative of Dr. Baer's investment of so much time and thought, I hasten to reassure him about one point that was of considerable concern to him: No, I would not rush in to establish an extinction procedure for his sneezing child. Not that I underestimate the power of learning approaches! Nor am I especially callous concerning the possible negative social consequences of a strong sneezing habit. No, my reasons are different: The latest since Bell's (1968) paper on the "bidirectionality of effects," but even dating back to my studies of the ethologists N. Tinbergen and K. Lorenz, I would not have rushed to the assumption that the mother was the causative agent. In contrast, I would have presumed that the chances are equal that either the child or the mother might be the causative agent in this interaction and that, most probably, each would affect the other. Being led by this presumption to a skeptical *epoché*, I would have continued observing the phenomena for a considerable time, subjecting any conclusion to a prolonged "suspension of conviction" (E. Husserl). In due course, I would have noticed that the child sometimes engaged in a sneezing sequence in the absence of the mother and other adults and that she was consequently not "reinforced" for it, but that she did not exhibit any signs of disappointed expectations by listening or visually searching for the expected reinforcing person. Having become even more skeptical, I would have noticed after the course of a few weeks, i.e., with the child's recovery from her cold, that the sneezing episodes declined suddenly in frequency and then stopped almost completely despite the very frequent preceding "reinforcement" from the mother's side. At this point, I would have begun to suspect that there might exist other causative agents for sneezing besides maternal reinforcement.

Expressed in more technical terms and less post hoc, the answer might be even more assuring: Very effective methodologies exist to avoid an incorrect and premature conclusion. The careful study of the patterns of transitional probabilities, as employed in the present project, would first help to decide whether the hypothesized contingency pattern is really as frequent and consistent as a preliminary impression might have suggested. Additionally, extensive evaluations of whether the transitional probabilities, and therefore the patterns, are stationary (as discussed in detail in the main study) would almost certainly have prevented the incorrect hypotheses feared by Dr. Baer. If time series analyses are added to these two methodologies, as planned for the very near future in the case of the present project, the danger of misinterpretations and premature conclusions is even further decreased. All of these methods would have shown a decrease of either the item in question or of the patterns suspected to be the causal ones. Since both individual items and patterns would have been seen to decrease, no careful researcher would postulate cause-effect relationships between maternal verbal response and the sneezing frequency, even in the absence of any experimental approaches.

Turning to the question whether the experiment is the ultimate methodology in psychology, it can not be attempted to do justice to this complex problem. Beginning with the work of Brunswick (1955, 1956), many excellent analyses (Willems, 1968; Pereboom, 1971; Snow, 1974; Bronfenbrenner, 1979) have compared experimental and observational methodologies. But being skeptically inclined, I shall mention at least some doubts in regard to the present project: I fully agree that my present study does not aim at a definitive exploration of cause-effect relationships and that many challenges exist to proceed above and beyond my analyses. But I am somewhat wary about waiting for experimental approaches to provide the conclusive answers. To disentangle the multiple cause-effect relationships of my 76 variables of instructional techniques alone might prove somewhat difficult for the experimentalist. I am further aware of almost certain multiple causation and of possible catalytical effects, so that one antecedent only leads to a subsequent behavior if another one preceded or accompanied it in setting the stage. I also suspect considerably delayed effects and other unknown complications. I therefore wonder whether I might not as well proceed with my less than perfectly unambiguous methods of probabilistic and correlational analyses. These methods might not be decisive, but they will provide a rich set of hypotheses and insights into the intricacies of the interrelationships. The latter seem to have been too formidable up to now for the experimentalist even to tackle them with his relatively simplistic methods. Only complex multivariate approaches, with careful attention being paid to Brunswick's precautions against artificially tying and untying of variables, to his call for ecological validity and for probabilistic approaches, might provide the tools sophisticated and complex enough to account for the intricate dynamics of the observed phenomena. Such designs would, however, be a far cry from the simple beauty of the "functional proof" advocated by Dr. Baer.

While certainly acknowledging the potential contributions of many diverse methodologies, as long as they are discerningly matched with the tasks at hand and carefully analyzed, I nevertheless wonder in my more audacious moments whether experimental approaches are not singularly unsuited when phenomena of considerable complexity are to be studied and when a field is first to be charted in its multiple dimensions. Experimental designs reflect mainly the conceptual apparatus of the experimenter, which in the past has often been very narrow, being confined to reinforcement, punishment, extinctions, and few other variables. Reality, in contrast, might harbor phenomena and exhibit relationships the experimenter never has dreamed of and which he therefore could not incorporate into his designs.

Research on first language acquisition and teaching is certainly a complex field and still in its early stages. Therefore it still lacks complete and generally accepted taxonomies of the phenomena of importance. Even if it should be agreed upon that experiments can provide the *ultimate* (taken in a temporal sense) proof for questions of cause-effect relationships, they might just therefore be ill fitted as *primary* (again temporal) methods for the exploration and description of partly unknown phenomena.

REFERENCES

Bell, R. Q. A reinterpretation of the direction of effects in studies of socialization. *Psychological Review*, 1968, 75, 81–95.

Bronfenbrenner, U. *The ecology of human development. Experiments by nature and design*. Cambridge, Mass.: Harvard University Press, 1979.

Brunswick, E. Representative design and probabilistic theory in a functional psychology. *Psychological Review*, 1955, 62, 193–217.

Brunswick, E. *Perception and the representative design of psychological experiments*. Berkeley: University of California Press, 1956.

Pereboom, A. C. Some fundamental problems in experimental psychology: An overview. *Psychological Reports*, 1971, 28, 439–455.

Snow, R. E. Representative and quasi-representative designs for research on teaching. *Review of Educational Research*, 1974, 44, 265–291.

Willems, E. P. An ecological orientation in psychology. In N. S. Endler, L. R. Boulter, & H. Osser (Eds.), *Contemporary issues in developmental psychology*. New York: Holt, Rinehart & Winston, 1968.

Commentary on Dr. Moerk's Response

Donald M. Baer

Prudence in the interpretation of correlations is certainly to be commended, and Dr. Moerk has indeed displayed a commendable prudence in his monograph. My first point here is simply to recommend even more prudence in this matter, by reminding us all of the phenomena seen in the analysis of reinforcement schedules. It is now a commonplace in operant conditioning to acknowledge that an operant response may be reinforced according to an extremely wide variety of patterns, and that particular choice among these patterns can yield virtually any rate of the reinforced response, almost any pattern of its occurrence over time, and *any apparent correlation with its solely functional reinforcer*, from near zero to near 1.00, that we might wish. The prudent tactics that Dr. Moerk has just described might sometimes cause the disclaimer of the reinforcer as the reinforcer, in many of those schedules. Yet some of those schedules seem likely to characterize many human interactions, and in any event, the reinforcer *is* the functional agent in them (and ought not to be disclaimed).

I agree completely with the thesis that in the absence of better techniques, we will do well to proceed with these techniques; otherwise I could not have commended Dr. Moerk's study as enthusiastically as I have. My point is only to suggest that we also try to move on from there.

I can see that the *apparent* complexities of the cases that Dr. Moerk has studied seem forbidding to the notion of simplistic experimental analysis. I cannot answer directly, but I can retreat to a metaphor, one suggested by Lewis Thomas in an essay on the nature of medical research (1979). Thomas points out that tuberculosis was not long ago thought to be a very complex disease, involving apparently five different organ systems, and relating (in weak correlations) to an exceptionally wide variety of environmental and hereditary circumstances. Then it was discovered that its cause was a certain bacillus, and suddenly it was a very simple disease. All those correlations were relevant to conditions that contributed a little to the probability of encountering the bacillus and a little to the probability of being able to resist it when it was encountered. But control of the tuberculosis reduced quite simply to control of the bacillus: medications that kill the bacillus cure the disease; social conditions that militate against the bacillus (which include the successful cure of present cases) prevent the disease. Now, Thomas says, it is neither a complicated nor interesting disease for medical research.

Is it possible that the causal agencies in the phenomena that Dr. Moerk is studying are not so complicated as they seem in the absence of knowing about their bacillus? Is it possible that their bacillus is the social reinforcement contingency? If so, the experimental analysis of that contingency may not be so complex—it has been done elsewhere in real-life interactions and in manageable ways. If not, then Dr. Moerk's prudence, and his reluctance to apply simplistic experimental tactics to nonsimplistic mechanisms, are choice strategies of inquiry. My recommendation was only to gamble a little, but from a position of prudence. I still believe that that position is all the sounder because of Dr. Moerk's efforts in this research.

REFERENCE

Thomas, L. *The medusa and the snail*. New York: Viking Press, 1979.

Author Index

Numbers in *italics* indicate where a complete reference can be found.

Subject Index